No Other God

Words for the
Church today

To ~~Ivy~~

with love and blessings

from ~~Liz~~

By
Elizabeth Nice

Copyright © 2005 Elizabeth Nice
First published 2005 by Myrtle Books, 42 The Keep, Portchester, Hants PO16 9PR U.K.

All rights reserved. No part of this publication may be reproduced, stored in a retrieval system, or transmitted, in any form or by any means, electronic, mechanical, photocopying, recording or otherwise, without the prior permission in writing of the publishers.

Cover Design : Richard Nice
Printed by The Alpha Experience, 148 Kings Road, Newbury, Berkshire RG14 5RG

Unless otherwise indicated, all Scripture references are from the Holy Bible, New International Version (NIV), copyright ©, 1973, 1978, 1984 by the International Bible Society. Used by permission Hodder & Stoughton, a division of Hodder Headline.

Scripture quotations marked NKJV™ are taken from the New King James Version®, copyright ©, 1982 by Thomas Nelson, Inc. Used by permission. All rights reserved .

Scripture quotations marked RSV are taken from the Revised Standard Version of the Bible, copyright © 1946, 1952, and 1971 by the Division of Christian Education of the National Council of Churches of Christ in the USA. Used by permission. All rights reserved.

Scripture quotations from *"The Message"*, copyright © by Eugene H Peterson 1993, 1994, 1995, 2000, 2001, 2002. Used by permission of NavPress Publishing Group.

Acknowledgements

Very many thanks to the people who have helped and supported me in this project, not least of whom is my long-suffering husband Richard. A special thank you goes to him for his input on the text, in the art work and diagrammatic material and for his expertise in the technical and computing areas, but also for his constant prayer support, both in our weekly prayer times specifically dedicated to this project and at plenty of other times throughout the two years it has taken me to write it.

Thanks too to our son and daughter who have not only put up with the disruption to the household, but have always been supportive of Mum's efforts in the literary field, taken an interest in the progress of the project, been prepared to take on extra chores when I haven't had time to do them and have been ready with encouragement when I felt discouraged. Bless them both.

Thanks especially to Rev. Michael Cooper, our Parish priest and Rev. Sandy Mattheson for offering helpful comments as well as encouragement and to Brian Jerrard and Karen Morley for undertaking the arduous task of painstakingly proofreading the document. All the people throughout my circle of Christian friends, at church and elsewhere, who have taken an interest and added their support through prayer and encouragement, are too many to name individually here, but I am grateful to them all. Last but not least, thanks to Adam and his team who built me a lovely study to write in. Cheers lads, you "done good!"

Contents

Preface		1
The 'Words'		3
Chapter 1	*" What I want"*	9
Chapter 2	*" What I desire"*	25
Chapter 3	*" What I command"*	40
Chapter 4	*" What I ordain"*	55
Chapter 5	*" What I hate"*	73
Chapter 6	*Patterns in the **'Words'***	93
Chapter 7	*Who? ... 'Our God'*	105
Chapter 8	*What? ... 'The Truth'*	111
Chapter 9	*Why? ... 'For the sake of - '*	120
Chapter 10	*How? ... 'To the Glory of God'*	126
Chapter 11	*Absent Fathers*	132
Chapter 12	*Abundance*	144
Chapter 13	*Control*	155
Chapter 14	*Renewal*	167
Chapter 15	*Rebellion*	179
Epilogue		191
Bibliography		

Every Chapter is sub-divided into sections of no more than two pages, with each section starting on a new page. Chapters 1 to 5 contain nine very short sections each, plus an introduction and a story. Chapters 6 to 15 comprise of an introduction and six slightly longer sections. All sections have a sub-heading and quotes to focus on, from the prophetic words I received, coupled with Bible references, or from the stories. I have divided it up into 'bite-size' chunks like this in order to allow people as much flexibility in using the book as possible. It can be read straight through or dipped into. Alternatively it could be used for personal or group study, maybe by taking one, or several sections a day and covering one Chapter a week. As I suggested on the back cover, the first five Chapters of basic commentary on the *'Words'* would be very suitable for a Lent course.

So that there may be no confusion, wherever I use the terms *'Words'*, or *'Word'*, I am referring not to the Bible, which is often called The Word, or the Word of God, but to the sets of prophetic words I received from the Lord as the basis of this book. These *'Words'* are set out in their entirety, immediately after the Preface. Then at the start of each of Chapters 1 to 5 I have repeated the set of *'Words'* belonging specifically to that Chapter.

For those who would find it helpful, here is a sample page layout, explaining what's what :-

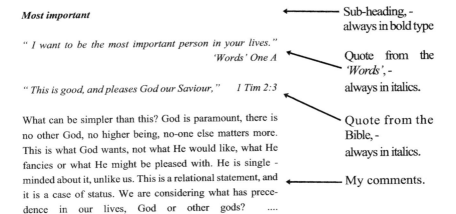

PREFACE

In the summer of 2001 I was pottering about in my kitchen getting the family dinner, saying my prayers as I did so - not because my cooking is so atrocious you understand! I had received my commission from the Lord to be a writer for Him in the January of that year and I had tried out a few preliminary ideas. I was praying about what to do next. The Lord very clearly told me to write about *'What I want'*; *'What I desire'*; *'What I command'*; *'What I ordain'*; and *'What I hate'*, *I* meaning Him. This decided, I engaged entirely with the task of cooking dinner. The next day, I jotted down that list, adding on a few more that seemed to me to be readily associated with it. Before long I had turned the original instructions into an idea of my own, to write something about knowing God's will. Then the school holidays intervened and I had to put writing aside in favour of entertaining the family.

When September came and they all returned to various educational establishments, I cleared the mile high pile off my desk and retrieved my notes, addressing the issue with serious intent. Three days later I dried up. I carried on trying, assuming all I needed was to persevere in the face of adversity. All I achieved was to confuse myself, so I took a break and cleaned the house. This got me round to Monday morning again. During the break, my mind would have cleared I was sure. This time though, I did what I should have done the week before. I prayed before I started writing. Well, that's not strictly how it was. I did pray the week before. The difference the second week was that I didn't shoot up an arrow prayer then get down to it. I sat back in my chair, closed my eyes and focused on God, opening up to His Spirit and asking Him to show me what to write.

I would understand if He had been a bit peeved with me, but not so. "I have told you what to write," He said gently. "You are to write about what I want, what I desire, what I command, what I ordain and what I hate. Those five and nothing else." Woops. There went my idea of writing about knowing God's will. *Where* had I got that from anyway? So that is what I did and this book is the result.

There are, as you will see, five sets of prophetic *'Words'*, one for each of the things identified by the Lord, which I received directly from Him over the next six to eight weeks. Some were almost dictated word for word, for others I had to wait before the Lord and work at them until I got the finished text and structure correct. They were confirmed as from the Lord by other Christian witness and by checking them against scripture, before I decided what to do with them. I knew they were for a wider audience than my own home church. In fact as I meditated on them, it became crystal clear that they are God's *'Words'* to the whole of His church, worldwide. I started working on a framework for an exposition of the *'Words'* and saw that the book falls into three distinct parts. These have remained as the underlying structure. Chapters 1 to 5 are a brief commentary on the *'Words'*, linking them to specific Bible passages. Each of these Chapters is accompanied by a short story illustrating the main theme of the set of *'Words'* for that chapter. Chapters 6 to 10 are more interpretative and the last five Chapters contain themed material, based on the stories that accompany each set of *'Words'* . Although inevitably, there is overlap and some repetition, I have endeavoured to avoid the latter as far as I can, to prevent tedium, but some things just have to be repeated, they are so important and critical to the overarching notion, that we, the church of God, His people, must have no other God but Him.

I offer this book to you then, in the prayerful wish that these *'Words'* will open your eyes as they have mine, to the incredible love our God has for us all and to His true purposes for His church here on earth. As I received and wrote down the *'Words'* it felt like handling a bolt of electricity, without the fatal side-effects, and I hope it is the same for you. With my husband I have trembled and even wept at what I have been led to write, but through it all, the thread of God's glory, triumph and victory runs so strongly that you can only finish up lost in wonder and praise. Our God is truly awesome. His power is boundless, beyond anything we can know or imagine. Let Him speak to you through this book and draw you ever closer to Him, so that His will for you, and for His church, may not only be done, but may be seen to be done by all the world . Amen. Glory be to God.

THE 'WORDS'

Introduction

Briefly, before we begin I want to make clear that the *'Words'* contained in this Chapter were given to me by the inspiration of the Holy Spirit and that in no way are they my own ideas or opinions. I have set them out all together here in this first Chapter for two reasons. One, to establish the foundation of the book from the outset, and second, for your convenience as the reader.

Set One   *'What I want'*

A) "I want to be the most important person in your lives.
    I want mankind everywhere to lift up holy hands and worship Me."

B) "I want all men to know My love, My care, My salvation.
    I want to shower you with My blessings."

C) "I want My people to turn from their selfish, sinful ways, to turn back to Me.
    I want to bless you, My people and be with you always, everywhere."

D) "I want to pour out My Spirit on you so that you can be My messengers, stewards and ambassadors in the world.
    I want My church to reverberate with My praise and My power so that the world sits up and takes notice."

Set Two   *'What I desire'*

A)   "I desire a romantic relationship with each one of you, My children. I long to be as intimate with you as the very air you breathe."

B)   "I rejoice over you with singing. My delight is in you and you are desirable to Me.
I long to adorn you with the adornments of My love, with gifts and garments, graces and a new name known only to Me."

C)   "I am an aggressive lover, pursuing you, My beloved children, across the plains of Earth and Heaven, seeking to save, redeem, protect and nurture you.
I am deeply hurt when you are indifferent to My love and careless of My affection"

D)   "I long for you to reject all your other lovers and to remember your first love for Me, so that I can gather you close into My arms and whisper My endearments to you.
Above all else I desire you with all My heart and long for you to desire Me with all your heart."

The 'Words'

Set Three   *'What I command'*

A)   *"I have said I want to be first in your lives, to be the most important person to you.*
       My command is that you have no other God but Me."

B)   *"I have given you My word, the Holy Scriptures, and My Word, My Son Jesus Christ.*
       I expect you to obey them both, willingly and lovingly."

C)   *"I command you to keep yourselves holy, to keep your lives free from worldly taints, to live by My statutes, laws and decrees.*
       In this way the world will see who I am and will understand My message."

D)   *"I do not want to frighten you or oppress you with harsh, impossible demands, as worldly masters do. I love you.*
       I am your Heavenly King and Master, there is no other God but Me."

E)   *"My law is absolute, I made it, I alone, to achieve My purposes, none other, and it is good.*
       Walk in it and you will prosper and know peace."

Set Four   ***"What I ordain"***

A)   *" My church .... to reflect My Glory in the world."*

       " How little of My glory shines out from your churches. How much of your paltry glory masks My wonderful glory, when you pursue worldly ends instead of heavenly ones."

B)   *" My people .... to share My love with the world."*

       " Where are the prophets, teachers, evangelists and missionaries for this age?"

C)   *" My Son .... to bring salvation to the world."*

       " Why are you whispering when you should be shouting the Good News?"

D)   *" My word .... to feed the hungry of the world."*

       " Why are you so preoccupied with the social when you you should be focused on the spiritual?"

E)   *" My creation .... to satisfy My love."*

       " How is it that I look for the fulfilment of My creation and I do not see it?"

The 'Words'

Set Five "What I hate"

A)   "I hate injustice. I am a God of mercy, requiring mercy. You know that I love all mankind, that I have made all people equal. Any oppression or inequality is unjust and offends against My good and perfect law."

B)   "I hate indifference. Too often you have been indifferent to the sufferings of others, both near to you and far off, but worse, far worse than this is your indifference to Me, to My gifts, to My word and to My Spirit. Warm your hearts, warm your spirits, fan into fire the flames of passionate love for Me, for My Word and for My world."

C)   "I hate your compromises. My truth is absolute. I have made that clear to you. My word is founded on My truth. If you think you do not know what the truth is, then you need to know My word, to look for the truth, as I have given it to you, in Scripture. It is there, plain for you to see, but you do not look for it. You prefer to use the easy premises of the world, that are based on erroneous thinking. Read, learn, know and live My truth, and it will set you free, free from the tyrannous power of the world."

D)   "I hate materialism. Take care that you have godly concern for the use of your money and possessions. Where I bless you with worldly wealth, I do it so that you can do more for Me. I do not give it only for your comfort and certainly not to confer superior status on you. I do it to enable you to spread My gospel and to proclaim My love to all the people I bring within your circle of influence, some very close to you, right where you are living, as well as others further away from you."

E) "I abhor hypocrisy, the whited sepulchre of religious pride, the sin that has beset and spoiled too much of the work of My church here on earth. I love to receive the praises of My children as they worship Me with hands and arms raised high, but why are so few of you willing to seek My forgiveness on your knees, even flat on your faces, so that I might forgive and raise you up to walk even more upright lives, pleasing and serving Me and fulfilling the deepest desires of your own hearts?"

F) "I hate defeatism. My church is the Church triumphant, victorious. I am not dead, Christianity is not dead. I am very much alive and My followers have life, abundant life, and joy, deep wells of joy, bubbling up in their spirits, bubbling up and spilling over, out into the world around them. Spilling out and always being refilled, refilled from the never-ending source that is Me. How can you walk in defeat when I have given you feet to skip lightly in blissful joy through this life and all its troubles? Shake off your feeling of defeat My children. Lift up your heads, lift up your eyes and see My triumph, see My victory and know that we can never, never be defeated. Amen, so be it. As I have spoken, so shall it be. Hallelujah!"

CHAPTER 1

" WHAT I WANT "

The 'Words'

A)   *"I want to be the most important person in your lives.*
I want mankind everywhere to lift up holy hands and worship Me."

B)   *"I want all men to know My love, My care, My salvation.*
I want to shower you with My blessings."

C)   *"I want My people to turn from their selfish, sinful ways, to turn back to Me.*
I want to bless you, My people and be with you always, everywhere."

D)   *"I want to pour out My Spirit on you so that you can be My messengers, stewards and ambassadors in the world.*
I want My church to reverberate with My praise and My power so that the world sits up and takes notice."

Introduction

1 Tim 2:1-8

"I urge, then, first of all, that requests, prayers, intercession and thanksgiving be made for everyone - for kings and all those in authority, that we may live peaceful and quiet lives in all godliness and holiness. This is good, and pleases God our Saviour, who wants all men to be saved and to come to a knowledge of the truth. For there is one God and one mediator between God and men, the man Christ Jesus, who gave himself as a ransom for all men - the testimony given in its proper time. And for this purpose I was appointed a herald and an apostle - I am telling the truth, I am not lying - and a teacher

of the true faith to the Gentiles. I want men everywhere to lift up holy hands in prayer, without anger or disputing."

This first set of *'Words'* is God's policy document, His statement of intent, not just for the rest of the *'Words'* but for all His work. In 1 Tim 2:1 - 8, the parallel Bible passage for *Set One* of the *'Words'* Paul, speaking for God, outlines what he wants to see in the church - men and women behaving appropriately while they praise, worship, pray and minister together to bring God's word to the world, which is exactly what *Set One* is all about. This passage contains plenty of material to mesh with this *'Word',* as we shall see. God is making His wishes crystal clear . *'I want mankind .... I want all men .... I want My people ... I want My church. '* This is not the whining of the spoilt child. Hear the yearning in God's voice. This is the desperate longing of the most sovereign authority, over His created people to whom He gave free will. Free will to turn to Him, or turn away. When we do turn away, which, let's be honest, we often do, how He longs to have us back.

These first five chapters of commentary, you will find, are fairly brief. They are my initial thoughts and ideas, and do not, in any way, deal with every detail found in the *'Words'*. This is a deliberate strategy, to allow you, the reader, plenty of scope for exercising your own thinking, prayers about and meditations on the *'Words'*. Just pause and roll them round in your mind until you're revelling in them, soaking them up, filled with them. Don't they call for a response from you? When someone you love pleads for you as God does here, don't you turn to them in loving response? This is precisely what God wants.

CHAPTER 1   *" WHAT I WANT "*

Most important

" I want to be the most important person in your lives."   'Words' One A

" For there is one God and one mediator between God and men, the man Christ Jesus."   1 Tim 2:3

What can be simpler than this? God is paramount, there is no other God, no higher being, no-one else matters more. This is what God wants, not what He would like, what He fancies or what He might be pleased with. He is single-minded about it, unlike us. This is a relational statement, but also it is a case of status. We are considering what has precedence in our lives, God or other gods? Who or what do we care about most? This is about making Him sovereign in our lives and the spin off is, the more important we make Him, the more He can bless us and use us. Therefore, just as He has made His declaration of intent, so we need to make our decision, to establish the fundamental principle in our lives that God has prime importance. This is an issue we cannot ignore or relegate. It has to be resolved. If you know that God is not of paramount importance to you and that something else is, no matter how worthy, then you need to correct this. Waste no more time, just do it. *" This is good, and pleases God our Saviour."* 1 Tim 2 : 3

All men

" *I want mankind everywhere........I want all men*"   *'Words'* One A, One B

" *[God] wants all men to be saved and to come to a knowledge of the truth.*"
1 Tim 2:4

I've extracted these two phrases from the *'Words'* in order to concentrate our attention on them. Paul uses a similar phrase -   " *who wants all men* ", *v 4*. No-one is left out. It is God's will that all people should be saved, in keeping with His loving and wholly benevolent nature. There is no discrimination. Salvation is available to absolutely every single human being who ever exists, regardless of race, colour, birth, attainment, status or any other ranking we may choose to put on them. We had better get a hold on that fact. All humans are created by God with the specific purpose of being His and living in relationship with Him.

As Christians we know that sin has broken that relationship and therefore necessitated our salvation. Non-Christians do not know this, but God wants them all to know it, which He stresses here by saying it twice. Firstly *"mankind"*, which is pretty all-inclusive adding *"everywhere"* to make it clearer still. Then He repeats it with *"all men"* so that we can be in no doubt of His intentions, as you would expect, given that we have said this first set of *'Words'* is His policy document. His first principle was to be the most important person in our lives. It is significant that His next stated principle is to do with others, not us.

CHAPTER 1   *" WHAT I WANT "*

The issue of holy hands

" lift up holy hands"   *'Words'* One A

" I want men everywhere to lift up holy hands "   *1 Tim 2:8*

Again Paul uses a similar phrase - *"I want men everywhere to lift up holy hands in prayer" v 8*. The *"men everywhere"* mentioned by Paul here are Christians throughout the church and he is using the generalised term *'people'* rather than the gender specific term for men alone. We can still see how closely the *'Words'* mirror the scriptures, not just here, but throughout.

So, what does this phrase, *'holy hands'* imply? I think immediately of the psalmists. David, in Psalm 24 asks *" Who may ascend the hill of the Lord?" v 3* and answers himself, *" He who has clean hands and a pure heart " v 4*. It is the reference to cleanliness that gives the best clue. Not the kind eschewed by schoolboys and conferred by soap and water, but the cleanliness obtained through inner, spiritual purity. The former type of cleanliness could be equated in spiritual terms with a Pharisaical obsession with legalistic observation of the law. Jesus however, told us that *" unless your righteousness surpasses that of the Pharisees and teachers of the law, you will certainly not enter the kingdom of heaven." Matt. 5:20*. This is demanding stuff. Who is this pure of heart? No-one, but the situation, as we shall soon see, is not hopeless.

There are many circumstances in which we would lift our hands. Worship, supplication, praise, thanksgiving, bringing requests before God are a few, similar to Paul's list of prayer types in v 1. The thing to note here is that the word used is active, we cannot be passive Christians.

The call to worship

" lift up holy hands and worship Me"   *'Words' One A*

" I want men everywhere to lift up holy hands in prayer, "   *1 Tim 2:8*

Nothing particularly difficult or challenging here. The church bells ring on a Sunday morning and the faithful [few] assemble for worship, faithfully. Worship having duly been done, they all depart again to their good Sunday lunch and the rest of the week, secure in the certainty that their duty has been fulfilled.

If your concept of worship is as limited as this, then hang on to your seat, you're in for a rough ride. Listen to this, it's Paul again :- *" I urge you, brothers, in view of God's mercy, to offer your bodies as living sacrifices, holy and pleasing to God - this is your spiritual act of worship." Romans 12:1* Not a single mention of Liturgy, Parish Communion, Matins or any other church service that might occur on a Sunday morning. "I worship at St Whoever's" does not necessarily equate with true worship. Individual cases will differ, but too often "I worship at ...." simply means "I attend ".

We are being called to worship, not just to attend church a little more frequently. This, as with the issue of holy hands, is demanding stuff. We need to understand what this word worship really means. We need to cast off our half-baked notions about it and do it properly. It is sacrificial. Meditate on that. It is the crux of the matter.

CHAPTER 1   " WHAT I WANT "

To know His love, care and salvation

" I want all men to know My love, My care, My salvation."   'Words' One B

" God our Saviour, who wants all men to be saved and to come to a knowledge of the truth. For there is one God and one mediator between God and men, the man Christ Jesus, who gave himself as a ransom for all men"
1 Tim 2:3-6

Returning to 1 Timothy 2:4-6, we find another parallel with the *'Words'*. We'll be looking in more detail at the truth in Chapter 8, so here we're focusing on knowledge of God's love, care and salvation. Believers already do know them, but non-believers do not, or they may know something about them. This concerns God, and it must therefore concern us. God's loving care is so active in our lives, well, I know it is in mine. If you are not so sure, take a long, prayerful look at all the times you've been worried, had problems, been afraid or whatever, and, if you cannot discern the hand of God in those situations, ask Him to reveal it to you. He will and you'll just be amazed.

The trouble is, we over-use the word 'care', consequently it has lost its edge, but when God acts caringly, it is of a different dimension altogether. His care is a powerful dynamic at work forcefully throughout the world and down the centuries. The message of the cross may seem like foolishness to the unsaved, but to us, the saved, and to all who come into salvation, it is the manifestation of the power of God's love and care.

A shower of blessing

" I want to shower you with My blessings .... I want to bless you ...."
'Words' One B, One C

" I urge then, first of all, that requests, prayers, intercession and thanksgiving be made for everyone - for kings and all those in authority, that we may live peaceful and quiet lives in all godliness and holiness. This is good and pleases God our Saviour, who wants all men to be saved and to come to a knowledge of the truth. For there is one God and one mediator between God and men, the man Christ Jesus, who gave himself as a ransom for all men - the testimony given in its proper time. And for this purpose I was appointed a herald and an apostle - I am telling the truth, I am not lying - and a teacher of the true faith to the Gentiles."
1 Tim 2:1-7

The passage from Paul to Timothy is full of examples of what to expect as blessings from God, *'peaceful and quiet lives'*, *'to be saved'*, *'one mediator between God and men .... Jesus, who gave himself as a ransom for all men'*, even Paul himself, and all the others like him down the ages, *'a herald and an apostle, ... a teacher of the one true faith'*. We'll be covering *'Abundance'* later. For here, just absorb the fact that God is expressing His wish not to bless us, singularly, but to 'shower' us with blessings in the plural. Neither does He specify that only some people will be blessed. No-one is left out, we can all be showered, not haphazardly, like my bathroom is when my son has a shower, but deliberately, beneficially. The Bible is full of references to such showers, take just one instance, *Ezekiel 34:26 "I will send down showers in season; there will be showers of blessing."* This is the season of God's blessings. Are you standing ready to receive the shower?

CHAPTER 1   *" WHAT I WANT "*

The call to repentance

" I want My people to turn from their selfish, sinful ways, to turn back to Me."
'Words' One C

" I want men everywhere to lift up holy hands in prayer, without anger or disputing."
1 Tim 2:8

As we were called to worship earlier, so we are being called to repentance now. We have to face the unpalatable truth that, as Paul and John both say, we are all sinners and do fall short of what God intends us to be. Therefore there has to be a means of remedying this situation. God could say, "They're only human, I'll overlook their little peccadilloes. Any loving parent would," but that is not the loving way. Sin is not just a little peccadillo. Sin is harmful to our healthy spiritual growth, because it separates us irrevocably from God. Sin and holiness cannot mix. Therefore there has to be a process to deal with this ongoing problem and that process is repentance. Repentance has been described, very effectively I think, as a change of mind leading to a change of heart resulting in a change of direction. As you can see, it is far more than simply regretting or even saying sorry for a wrong action. A deliberate, transforming act is being called for here, not just a token effort - 'I will repent of this, fully. In other words, I admit it, I regret it, I turn from it and I will have nothing more to do with it whatsoever. I will also do all I can to repair any damage to others caused by my sinfulness and I will move on into a deeper walk with God, wherever He takes me. '

God's presence

> "*I want to .... be with you always, everywhere.*"
>   'Words' One C

> "*For there is one God and one mediator between God and men, the man Christ Jesus*"
>   1 Tim 2:5

Set One is building to its climax now. Like a preacher, God has got into the swing of it. This is an impassioned plea for us to draw close to God so that He can draw closer to us. We're being asked to stop shutting Him out of our lives and involve Him completely, right down to the smallest details. After all, He has declared He wants to be the most important person to us. You don't *ex*clude such a person from your life, you *in*clude them. Notice too that this little clause qualifies the preceding comment, '*I want to bless you, My people.*' Being with us, always and everywhere is an integral part of God's blessing. If this gives you the uncomfortable feeling that you have to keep looking over your shoulder to see if God is watching you, then what are you doing that you don't want Him to see? A policeman friend of ours once said to my son 'If you're not doing anything wrong, you've got nothing to be afraid of have you?' But God is not a policeman. He longs to enfold us, permanently, in His mantle of protection and care. I find it immensely comforting to know He is there in all the trials of life, and He wants us all to feel that.

Chapter 1   " What I Want "

So that

" I want to pour out My Spirit on you so that you can be My messengers .... "
" I want My church to reverberate .... so that the world sits up and takes notice."   'Words' One D

[pray] " for kings and all those in authority, that we may live peaceful and quiet lives in all godliness and holiness."   1 Tim 2:2

I'm looking at the conjunctions here rather than the thought content, the words *'so that'*. This refrain runs right through the *'Words'*. One thing occurs in order that another may obtain. Here, God acts or requires action, in order to have an effect on the world. Elsewhere, He asks for certain attitudes or behaviours on our part, in order that we may receive a benefit. Using this little refrain we can ask ourselves a very important question :- *'Why should we have no other God?'* - and answer it :- *so that* the world may believe.

God wants to pour out His Spirit on us, His church, impacting on the world so that it *'sits up and takes notice'* of the message of salvation. You will see in *Set Five* that our wealth comes under this stricture too. We are endowed with wealth - so that - we can do more for God. There is a 'so that' in Paul's words to Timothy, v 2 and Paul infers that his appointment, as a herald, an apostle and a teacher, v 7, was made so that others may be won for Christ.

In *Set Two*, we are urged to reject our *'other lovers'* - *so that* - God can gather us close into His arms and whisper His endearments to us. Similarly, in *Set Five*, God tells us to warm our hearts - *so that* - we can *'fan into fire the flames of passionate love'* for Him. There could be no better place to end this Chapter, in readiness for moving on to contemplate *Set Two* of the *'Words'*, - *'What I desire'*, than with this exhortation to be more loving towards our heavenly Father.

Before we do however, there is the story that accompanies this first set of *'Words'* to be read and pondered over. What is the purpose of this story? How does it help us in our meditations on the *'Words'*?

Story 1)   **2 K. B.**

Netta was feeling really nervous that morning. So much that she felt sick and couldn't face her breakfast. Six years old and starting a new school. Her old one had not satisfied her Mum and Dad, so they had moved her to this new one. She was going to be in class 2 K. B. The teacher was a Mrs Brown.

Netta knew nothing about Mrs Brown, nor about the other children in class 2 K. B. Gripping her Mum's hand tightly, and the strap of her new backpack with the other hand, Netta trotted to school and took her place in 2 K. B.'s straggly line of children in the playground.

Mrs Brown looked friendly as she walked down the line greeting each child and saying hello to those Mums, or Dads, who were there. When she got to Netta her smile grew.

"Are you Tansy Smith or Netta Jones?" she asked.

"Netta," the little girl whispered.

"Good girl. Well, I'm Mrs Brown. Welcome to our school Netta. Is this your Mum?"

Netta's Mum was hovering anxiously.

"Yes, I'm her Mum."

Mrs Brown shook hands with her.

"I'm very glad to meet you. I can't talk now at any great length, as you will realise, with all the children to look after, but please don't hesitate to come in and see me at any time if you've any worries about Netta or if any problems occur."

Netta's Mum nodded seriously, then turned to Netta and gave her a twinkly little smile.

"Go on darling, in you go. You'll be alright."

The line of children moved off and Netta went with them, with one swift backward glance at her Mum, who smiled and waved encouragingly.

By the end of the day Netta had firmly decided she liked Mrs Brown and had made friends with two other girls. It looked as though this new school was going to be good. The other two girls said Mrs Brown was a lovely teacher, one had an older sister who'd been in Mrs Brown's class two years ago and

Chapter 1   "What I Want"

had loved it. They believed this happily. For Netta it was a bigger step of faith, but she felt she could take it and she was to find that Mrs Brown would not disappoint her.

Mrs Brown had spent the first part of the morning outlining the projects they were going to study that year. They sounded really exciting to Netta. She couldn't wait to get started on them. The classroom looked inviting too. The one at her old school had been tatty and neglected, everything shambolic and untidy. This one was clean and bright with lots of exciting artifacts and interesting pictures. When Netta needed a pencil they were easy to find in a clearly marked wooden block on the shelf, just as anything else the children might need was set out for them. They didn't have to search fruitlessly through cupboards and drawers for things, as they had at her last school, only to find, if they did locate what they were looking for, that it was broken, empty or incomplete.

Mrs Brown outlined a few simple rules for the classroom and invited the children to comment on them or suggest any others they thought should be added. Netta was surprised at how confidently the other children discussed this and how Mrs Brown listened and took notice of what they were saying. Her previous teacher had shouted orders continuously over the babble and racket and no-one had taken much notice. She certainly never listened if any child commented on her instructions. Most days Netta came home complaining of a headache and it was this that had alerted her Mum and Dad to the problems and decided them eventually to change her school.

For Sam Paulson, it was a slightly different picture. He had been asked to leave his last school after a series of incidents that culminated in another child being quite badly hurt. Sam was sorry, really, but the silly boy had deserved it, he felt. Sam's Mum had threatened him with every dire punishment she could think of if he started playing up at this new school! He was lucky to get a place there, she told him. It was much better than his old one. It had cost her more than just money to get him in there. She'd had to move house in order to live near enough and that had meant uprooting them from the neighbourhood where all her family and friends lived. Sam's Dad had left them some years ago and Sam never saw him now. His Mum was always reminding him that she had to be Mum and Dad to him, so that was why she was so strict. Sam could understand that, but he did resent it, especially when he saw other boys being given more freedom and more material possessions than he was allowed.

As he took his place in the 2 K. B. line, without his Mum's support on the sidelines because she had to go to work, he silently assessed the look of the other children. Although better dressed and cleaner than most of his old classmates, they didn't seem terribly friendly and they were amazingly obedient! The children at his old school never lined up in this docile way, in spite of all the screaming and harrying of teachers and assistants.

The woman who was their teacher was advancing on him with a soppy smile on her face. In six short years Sam had quickly learnt that soppy smiles generally evaporated like snow in the sun after a few minutes acquaintance with him! He glowered at the woman, waiting to see this happen. She just met his eyes and held them for a second or two.

"You're Sam. Hello," she said, continuing to look at him, not smiling any more but still friendly. "I'm Mrs Brown."

"Hello," he grunted.

She passed on down the line to where Netta waited. The morning passed slowly for Sam with a lot of boring talk. He wanted to explore some interesting looking drawers labelled 'Space Builder' and 'Polydrons'. In the afternoon they had to do some writing and drawing, after a short little Maths test, which was so easy Sam wondered if he'd been put in the wrong class. The other children on the table Mrs Brown had allocated him to were really excited about the writing and drawing task and talked about it all the time they were doing it. Sam sat back and watched in amazement, taking no part. They tried to include him, then gave up when he ignored them. He quickly did a page or two of writing on a subject that interested him, not the one Mrs Brown had set for them. Then he sat fiddling with his pencil, growing increasingly bored. After a minute or two, he decided to conduct an experiment. With a practised, sharp wrist action and a very satisfying snapping noise, he broke the pencil clean in two. The other boys looked up horrified. Sam grinned at

CHAPTER 1   " WHAT I WANT "

them unpleasantly, reached out for one of their pencils and repeated the action. The children at nearby tables had noticed by then and the room was growing tensely quiet.

Mrs Brown looked across at Sam's table and located the source of the tension, just in time to see him snap a third pencil. Sam's experiment was about to tell him what he wanted to know. What happens if ....? Mrs Brown called him over to where she was sitting, sorting out reading books with a group of children.

"Bring your writing Sam. I'd like to see what you've done," she said calmly. This threw Sam. It was not the response he'd been anticipating. Scowling deliberately, he snatched his exercise book up from the table, letting the broken pieces of the third pencil drop to the floor. He swaggered over to Mrs Brown and shoved the book onto the table in front of her, taking care to crease the pages. She gently smoothed them, then pulled out a vacant chair beside her and indicated he should sit on it. He did, nonplussed.

She then told the class to settle back to work and they all did, with a few covert looks at Mrs Brown and Sam. She read through Sam's writing then turned to him with a serious look.

"This is very good work Sam. Your spelling and handwriting are excellent, aren't they?"

Sam stared at her.

"Yes," he answered, defiantly. She didn't need to tell him that. He knew it. He was good at everything he chose to do. Still she said nothing about the pencils.

"Could you illustrate your work for me?" she asked. "I'd very much like to see what the aliens in your story look like."

Sam considered his response. Her hand rested on the back of his chair. Somehow he knew he was on a losing wicket if he tried to get up and return to the other table. She meant him to stay by her and she wasn't going to have any arguments about it. He shrugged and pulled the colouring pencils nearer to him. At the end of the lesson a boy from Sam's table brought the bits of broken pencil to Mrs Brown, wanting to know, very loudly, what he should do with them, giving Sam an accusing stare.

"Maybe Sam could answer that?" said Mrs Brown.

"I dunno," Sam shrugged.

"Put them in the bin please, Dean," she said decisively. "You've worked hard this afternoon Sam, and your work is excellent. I've already said that about your writing and I can see you're good at drawing too. How would you like me to reward you? Do you prefer stickers or shall I tell your Mum?"

Sam hadn't been listening to her, being too busy arrogantly ignoring her and sticking his tongue out rudely at the other children. His attention was jerked back when he heard the dreaded words 'tell your Mum'.

"I didn't mean it! I didn't mean to snap the pencils. They just broke. I went like that," he flicked his fingers gently, "and they just broke. Don't tell my Mum, she'll 'do' me!"

The surprise on Mrs Brown's face turned to careful assessment.

"So you're sorry you broke the pencils?"

"Yes, yes I am."

"O.K. You're forgiven. There will be no more said about it, but I must have your promise that you will not do it again."

"I won't. I promise," he said, too quickly.

"And you really mean that?"

"Yes I do," he replied a touch angrily.

"I accept your promise then. I shall hold you to it though. Now. Do you want a sticker for this work or do you want me to show it to your Mum?"

He gazed at her, realisation dawning. She'd tricked him! Tricked him into something he never did, on principle. Own up. Slumping back into the chair he mumbled sulkily "I'll have a sticker. My Mum won't be interested and she's not picking me up anyway."

With a puzzled frown Mrs Brown fetched her stickers and popped one onto his book. The class cleared away, went out to play, had a story and then it was home-time. Sam shot off as the bell went, pushing through the little groups of adults and children meeting each other in the playground. When he got back to the house his Mum wasn't there and it was all locked up. He left his bag on the back doorstep and roamed off to the play park nearby to amuse himself while he waited for her to come home from work.

CHAPTER 2
"WHAT I DESIRE"

The 'Words'

A)   "*I desire a romantic relationship with each one of you, My children. I long to be as intimate with you as the very air you breathe.*"

B)   "*I rejoice over you with singing, My delight is in you and you are desirable to Me.
I long to adorn you with the adornments of My love, with gifts and garments, graces and a new name known only to Me.*"

C)   "*I am an aggressive lover, pursuing you, My beloved children across the plains of Earth and Heaven, seeking to save, redeem, protect and nurture you.
I am deeply hurt when you are indifferent to My love and careless of My affection.*"

D)   "*I long for you to reject all your other lovers and to remember your first love for Me, so that I can gather you close into My arms and whisper My endearments to you.
Above all else I desire you with all My heart and long for you to desire Me with all your heart.*"

Introduction - 'O God of Love'

Song of Songs 8:6-7
"*Place me like a seal over your heart,
         like a seal on your arm;
for love is as strong as death,*

> *its jealousy unyielding as the grave.*
> *It burns like a blazing fire,*
> > *like a mighty flame.*
> *Many waters cannot quench love;*
> > *rivers cannot wash it away.*
> *If one were to give all the wealth of his house for love,*
> > *it would be utterly scorned."*

You will notice that each section of this Chapter has as its title the name of a hymn or song tune, some familiar, others less so. I chose them to lead in to the thoughts contained in each section and to enhance your meditations. I hope my strategy helps you.

Although at a first glance the layout and format of this second set of *'Words'* appears the same as the first, this set, as with all five sets, has its own distinctive character. One thing you will notice is that there is no mention of the world in this set. These four *'Words'* are specifically for believers. They are deeply personal and very moving. Some people may find them difficult or embarrassing, but I ask you not to avoid them, take your time, allow yourself to feel safe with them and let God minister to you through them. It is well worth it.

I have selected *Song of Songs* as the Bible passage to tie in with this *'Word'*, for fairly obvious reasons. In fact, the *Song* is sadly neglected in my opinion and this is to our detriment. A glance at its placing is interesting. Out of the 66 books of the Bible it is exactly the 22nd. For some, who are not fussed about numerology, this will be unimportant, but to me, it is where it is because God is saying "This is important, notice it. I have put an important message in it for you." Prior to it is all the history of the Fall, the flood, the Exodus, King David and so-on. Following it come some massive books of prophecy leading up to the events recorded in the New Testament. It marks a turning point in the Bible as a whole. It is a complex, difficult piece of writing, but it richly rewards close study. These two verses, 8:6-7 are recognised as a 'song within a song', a Hymn to Love. They are immensely powerful and eminently suitable to back up this second set of *'Words'*.

CHAPTER 2   *" What I Desire "*

'A Kind of Loving'

" I desire a romantic relationship with each one of you, My children. I long to be as intimate with you as the very air you breathe."   'Words' Two A

*" Place me like a seal over your heart,
like a seal on your arm;"*   Song 8:6a

We are left in no doubt as to precisely the kind of relationship God desires to have with us. It is very different to that which I was brought up to expect and possibly you could say the same. If you see God as **Almighty** God, powerful and unapproachable then what we are shown here will come as something of a surprise. It is unusual to associate the words *'romantic'* and *'intimate'* with God. Yet those are the words **He** chooses to use. Without being sexist I am aware that some men reading this may say, 'that's OK for her, she's a woman, but it isn't manly to feel that way. ' To any man who thinks like that, or to any woman who is having a problem with this I would like to pose a question. Do you not, deep in your heart of hearts, yearn for such intimacy? Wouldn't it at least be safer to accept intimacy with Him, than to deny your need for it, or seek it in less healthy sources?

All my childhood I went to Church, then I left home, started work and other things claimed my interest. My older sister faithfully persisted in witnessing to me about how God loved me and wanted a relationship with me. I couldn't understand that. Then one day I was at home with bronchitis, reading a Christian book she'd lent me, when I had a wonderful encounter with the Lord Jesus. It was as though He popped His head round the bedroom door, looking at me with such love that I was captivated by it. The room seemed to fill with a pure, beautiful light, invisible to the naked eye, but discernible to the spirit. I lay back with a huge sense of relief and said something like 'OK Lord, You can have me. I give myself to You. ' My life has never been the same and He has never left me since. Although everyone's experience of meeting the Lord is different, everyone can experience such a relationship with Him. He's very close, just waiting for you to open your heart to Him.

'Love Divine'

" I rejoice over you with singing, My delight is in you and you are desirable to Me".
'Words' Two B

*" Many waters cannot quench love;
rivers cannot wash it away"*
Song 8:7a

In my initial research for this section I came across a beautiful passage of scripture that I had no recollection of reading before. It is from Zephaniah Chapter 3, verse 17. *" He will take great delight in you, he will quiet you with his love, he will rejoice over you with singing."* It was experience of the same God who gave me these *'Words'* that inspired Zephaniah to write as he did. God intends His children to take comfort and encouragement from these thoughts. The image of God singing is extraordinary, yet wonderful. You may say it isn't actually God Himself singing, but that His delight in us is accompanied by heavenly singing - the angelic host who sang at Jesus' birth maybe. To me though, there stubbornly remains a picture of God, so thrilled with love for His people that He bursts into a spontaneous song of pure joy. David couldn't have stopped himself dancing for joy when the Ark of the covenant finally arrived at its proper resting place. God can no more stop Himself loving us. That He should then sing in expression of His love is entirely feasible. After all, we sing to express our love to Him and we are made in His image. Wow! What a God we have! There truly is none like Him, He chose us to be His children because He desires us so much and we are highly esteemed by Him.

CHAPTER 2   "*What I Desire*"

'All things bright and beautiful'

" *I long to adorn you with the adornments of My love, with gifts and garments, graces and a new name known only to Me*".   *'Words'* Two B

" *Hang my locket around your neck,
Wear my ring on your finger.*"   Song 8:6a *'The Message'*

Gifts, garments, grace and the promise of a new name all feature throughout the Bible. The giving of a name in Bible times gave an indication of such things as character, events or activity, particularly when they were remarkable in some way, bad as well as good. Getting a new name is exciting in itself. Women can be more privileged than the men in this respect, in that we change our surnames when we get married, handy if you've got a rotten one! Useful too, in signifying, to yourself and others, the change in your life, the break from old to new. What the Lord is saying here about a new name implies a whole new life, with Him, in His strength and joy and it is so special that He has created it and reserved it just for you and no-one else.

What also makes this *'Word'* so exciting is the language it's couched in. *"I long to ...."* God uses this plea four times in *Set Four* and nowhere else in the *'Words'*. Coupled with the reiterations of *"I want ...."* in *Set One* it gives a powerful sense of His yearning. The word *'adorn'*, and its derivative *'adornments'* convey a richness that surpasses the mere giving of gifts. We are enhanced by them. What is stopping Him then? There is without doubt a barrier of some sort, why else would He say that He longs to do so rather than simply doing it? My choice of Eugene Peterson's translation of the Song, verse 6 is deliberate. It echoes the feel of this *'Word'* so well and I repeat it here in reinforcement of God's plea :-

   "Hang my locket around your neck, Wear my ring on your finger."
Show the Lord, and the world, that you accept His adornments, that you are His.

'Wonderful love'

" I am an aggressive lover, pursuing you, My beloved children across the plains of Earth and Heaven".   'Words' Two C

" The fire of love stops at nothing -
It sweeps everything before it."   Song 8:6c 'The Message'

We finished the last section asking what are the barriers between us and God. We could sink into despair at this point. If there is such a block, how can God ever reach us? Well, this is how. He never gives up His pursuit of us. Christian literature refers to God as the Ageless Romancer, the Hound of Heaven, a wild Lover and the Pursuer to name but a few. Here, He dubs Himself *'an aggressive lover'*. Again, Peterson's translation gels so well with the *'Words'*. The image of the fire of God's love sweeping all before it is so powerful. Think of Elijah, scuttling off into a cave to escape his problems, only to find that God sent worse ones - wind, earthquake and then, fire! Having blown down, uprooted and finally burnt away Elijah's barriers, God had all his attention and only needed to use a still small voice to soothe him, reason with him and send him on his way. What happened to Paul, while he was still Saul? He was hot-footing it angrily to Damascus, to persecute the Christians there, totally unaware that he, in his turn was being pursued. A blinding light felled him and the rest, as they say, is history. There are no barriers too high, too wide or too strong to defeat our heavenly Lover in His pursuit of us. We matter too much to Him.

CHAPTER 2   " WHAT I DESIRE "

'My Saviour's Love'

" I am an aggressive lover, pursuing you, My beloved children across the plains of Earth and Heaven, seeking to save, redeem, protect and nurture you".   'Words' Two C

" love is as strong as death,
its jealousy unyielding as the grave"   Song 8:6b

In the last section we considered the idea of God pursuing us. What could be a greater pursuit than Jesus' saving action on the cross? The hymn that accompanies this tune starts with the words
> "I stand amazed in the presence of Jesus the Nazarene,
> and wonder how He could love me, a sinner, condemned, unclean.
> How marvellous! How wonderful! And my song shall ever be :
> How marvellous! How wonderful is my Saviour's love for me!"

The cross demonstrates for all time the cost of God's love, how far He is prepared to go to save and redeem us from the grip of sin. This is love of even greater quality than that described by Shakespeare in his Sonnet CXVI , that "bears it out even to the edge of doom". The love of God, in Jesus, did not stop at the edge, but went as far into the realms of doom as it is possible to go, defeated them and returned triumphant, all for our sake. It would be easy to read the *'Words'* casually, to glance over them, agree, because they do not tell us anything we are not already familiar with and go our way unaffected by them. They demand better than that. God is drawing our attention to what He has done for us and what He wants of us in such a way as to make us look at these things anew and make them our heartfelt concern.

'Love Unknown'

> " I am deeply hurt when you are indifferent to My love and careless of My affection." .
>
> 'Words' Two C

> " Love can't be bought, love can't be sold -
> It's not to be found in the marketplace."
>
> Song 8:7b 'The Message'

You cannot cheapen God's love, is the implication in Peterson's rendering and he is absolutely right. Not only would it be despicable to treat such an inestimable gift in such a way, but it also wounds the very heart of the person who loves us the most. Alex Buchanan wrote a book entitled "God has feelings too" in which the second chapter is headed 'A God who grieves'. In it he says "God grieves over today's church as much as he did over the seven churches in the province of Asia." The idea of God having feelings may be strange or new to you, but, as Buchanan states, He is a God "who does indeed feel grief, anger, joy and compassion. Who 'loves righteousness and hates iniquity ' ", who is not "an unfeeling and remote God".

If you 'put the boot on the other foot' for a minute and think how upset you are when someone rejects or ignores your love for them you will have an inkling of how God feels when we are indifferent to His love and careless of His affection for us. 'How are we indifferent and careless of Your love, Lord?' we may ask, rather like Malachi has the Israelites quizzing the Lord. There is a different answer for each one of us and it is for each of us to put this right in our own hearts with Him. There are also ways that the church as a whole has let God down and this is the main concern of this book.

CHAPTER 2   " WHAT I DESIRE "

'Passion Chorale'

" I long for you to reject all your other lovers and to remember your first love for Me".   *'Words' Two D*

" love is as strong as death, jealousy is cruel as the grave"   Song 8:6b RSV

Although under no circumstances can we call God cruel, we can call Him jealous. It is His own description of Himself ,*" I, the Lord your God, am a jealous God" Exodus 20 v 5.* As the NIV footnotes point out " God will not put up with rivalry or unfaithfulness." He has a perfect right to expect fidelity from His children. The notes continue " Actually, jealousy is part of the vocabulary of love." God's jealousy is not the same as the selfish human emotion, so destructive of relationships. God's jealousy is entirely preoccupied with securing His and our best interests.

There are echoes here of God's words to the church in Ephesus, the jewel in Paul's crown. *" I hold this against you : You have forsaken your first love. Remember the height from which you have fallen! Repent and do the things you did at first." Rev.2:4-5* Who was their first love? It was the Lord Himself. How could they have forsaken Him? The Lord is gentler with us. He restricts Himself to expressing a longing that we would reject all our other lovers and remember our first love for Him. When I think of the invective He could pour out on us for our neglect I tremble, but He does not want to punish us, which is really what we deserve. He longs to restore us to the kind of relationship He has always meant us to have with Him.

To finish this section, we have to ask ourselves, who or what, are our other 'lovers'? What preoccupies us to the exclusion of God?

'A Safe Stronghold'

" I long for you to reject all your other lovers and to remember your first love for Me, so that I can gather you close into My arms and whisper My endearments to you."   'Words' Two D

*" If one were to give all the wealth of his house for love,
It would be utterly scorned."*   Song 8:7b

> *"Were the whole realm of nature mine,
> that were an offering far too small;
> love so amazing, so divine,
> demands my soul, my life, my all. "*

So wrote Isaac Watts in the hymn 'When I survey the wondrous cross', which, incidentally is not the hymn that goes with the above tune. What have we got that we can give God in return for all that He has bestowed so freely and lovingly on us? Nothing, except ourselves.

Notice the *'so that'* here. Do you remember I said they occur when the Lord is at pains to show us that one thing must happen in order for something else to occur? For us to obtain such intimacy with Him, we must clean up our act, get rid of anything in our lives that we are putting before Him. Remember too that I said this set of *'Words'* is entirely personal. At this point we are talking about getting rid of 'other lovers' in our individual lives, so that the Lord can lift each one of us onto His knee and whisper His endearments into our ears only. It presents rather a ridiculous picture to imagine a church sitting on God's knee. Not being disrespectful, but I think the spire might get right up His nose!

CHAPTER 2   " WHAT I DESIRE "

'Sleepers, wake'

" Above all else I desire you with all My heart and long for you to desire Me with all your heart."   *'Words' Two D*

*" Place me like a seal over your heart,
Like a seal on your arm."*   Song 8:6a

T. S. Eliot penned the lines that, for me constantly mirror experience and are entirely appropriate here ;-

> *"We shall not cease from exploration
> And the end of all our exploring
> Will be to arrive where we started
> And know the place for the first time."*

We started with the Bible verse above and with the Lord's anguished plea for intimacy with us. Having seen the kind of lover He is and His right to expect our loyalty, fidelity and love in return, we come back to His impassioned cry for intimacy. How can we resist?

'Above all else'. This is the Creator God whose business is the running of the Universe. Yet above all that, above anything else He asks of us, He wants us for Himself, with *all* His heart. That is awesome when you really think what it means. What else can we do, but give Him all our hearts?

Again, before we move on to the next Chapter, there is another story to read. As you read it, consider it's relevance to the set of *'Words'* and ask yourself how it enhances and illustrates their message.

No Other God

Story 2)   ***Sammarah's Garden***

We will call her Sammarah, the woman he loves. Fickle, capricious, selfish and fearful, she broke his heart more often than she pleased him. Yet he stayed, always on the touch line of her life. Faithful. Loving her, longing for her real love in return, not just her craven attention when she needed comfort, support or advice. It was a mystery to his friends why he stayed with her, what he saw in her. They only saw the hardened exterior, albeit beautiful, but he knew the true beauty locked within, and he knew that he alone had the power to unlock that beauty, if she would grant him leave to do so.

"You are so lucky Sammarah," bemoaned one of her most long standing friends. "You have looks, money, possessions, brains and flair. I do envy you. What have I got? Nothing!"

"Nonsense," answers our heroine briskly. "You have it all too. You've got me for a friend."

Sammarah had just bought a property that gave her control over the water supply to an entire valley. She diverted this source of power and sustenance into the grounds of her own estate, to create a 'paradise garden' for people to enjoy. People, that is, of her own choice, acceptable to her.

The other residents of the valley do not feel so fortunate to have Sammarah nearby. They have access now to no more than a trickle of water and have resorted to other, less effective and very expensive means of obtaining water. This is fine for those who can afford to pay the exorbitant rates necessitated by such measures. Families who cannot find themselves in dire straits.

One such family consisted of a mother and her two children. The boy a difficult thirteen year old, his younger sister profoundly mentally and physically handicapped. The father long gone. For this family the need for water was paramount. Because of the sister, the mother could not work away from the home, so relied on their smallholding to provide their food, selling the surplus, scanty though it was, to fund other basic requirements. The boy seethed with resentments, against his absent father for deserting the mother and sister he loves fiercely, against the uncaring neighbours, against his better off, swanking peers, against the authorities and against himself for his power-

Chapter 2   "What I Desire"

lessness to help his mother. He is constantly in trouble. The authorities have run out of patience with him and deal with him harshly, when they can apprehend him, which only makes the situation worse and him angrier still. It is only a matter of time before he turns his anger on Sammarah, realising that she is the barrier to what he needs.

How does this happen? What is the flashpoint?

Before we can answer those questions we need to look further back, to the beginnings of Sammarah's relationship with Idral, the man who loved her so faithfully. He had always been there, as long as she could remember. A constant in a constantly shifting world as she grew up and moved around from home to home with her mother. One step-dad followed another in a blur. Who Idral was she had never been quite sure. As a child she had delighted to snuggle up close to him and hear his stories. As a teenager she had anticipated his visits for the quirky presents he brought her that always fitted the particular phase or fad she was currently preoccupied with. As a young adult, coming out into the world bolstered up by false confidence, his quiet support was always there to be counted on. From the secure base he supplied, she forayed out, engaging in passionate love affairs, taking up short-lived crusades for this issue or that 'wrong', throwing herself into scheme after scheme for making money. Every time things went wrong, she ran into his ever open arms and took his solace, freely offered, before turning away again to pursue a new diversion.

In time she became seriously wealthy and acquired her valley property. It was then that she fell out with Idral. He wanted her to share her 'paradise garden' freely with all and sundry. She would not. To her surprise, for the first time ever, her closest friend turned against her, siding with Idral. Sammarah turned on her coldly.

"You are weak, just as he is," she declared. "He has no idea how I've wound him round my little finger. I have the power, I only have to call and he comes running. But he's nothing more than a do-gooder, a hopeless idealist. His ideas are fine, perfect, in a perfect world but the world's not perfect, so they don't work and he can't see that. You're the same. No wonder you've got a weakness for him. You deserve him!"

Her friend, more used to backing down when Sammarah criticised her, found to her amazement that she could stand up to her.

"Oh no, Sammarah. You're wrong, so wrong. Idral's not my weakness. He's yours."

Ignoring her friend's words Sammarah continued with her project.

Predictably, the little family in the valley hit a major crisis. The mother collapsed, having given the best of what food they had to the boy and his sister. The boy struggled to look after them both but it was too much for him and his sister died. His resentment erupted and he ran amok through the valley, terrifying residents and destroying property indiscriminately. Eventually he arrived at the main gate to Sammarah's garden. His anger cooled to an icy fury as the full implications of what she had done dawned on him. The gates of course, were firmly locked against unwanted intruders. This did not deter the boy. He knew of other, illegal ways into the garden. His intentions steeled now, he slipped in through one of these and went in search of Sammarah. Soon he spotted her, resting languidly on the terrace, entertaining a select group of acquaintances. Letting out a manic howl of anguish, the boy raced across the lawn and fell upon her, screaming, hitting, biting, scratching and kicking. The guests scattered in horror and stood watching transfixed as her pristine white dress became blood splattered and her immaculate hair dishevelled. She fought him off with all her strength, but was losing the battle when Idral strode round the corner onto the terrace.

His voice was quiet yet powerful, commanding and authoritative.

"Stop that."

The boy turned to see who had addressed him in that way. Recognising a greater threat than he was posing at present, and holding Idral's eyes, he bent slowly, deliberately and withdrew a knife from where he had secreted it, strapped to his leg. A ripple of alarm ran through the onlookers. Sammarah was unable to see its cause as she was behind the boy, and she had her head in her hands, weeping. The boy whipped round meaning to act fast before someone unfroze enough to prevent him knifing her.

"If you do, you will never be able to forgive yourself," came Idral's quiet, steady voice.

Chapter 2   "What I Desire"

He made no move, his gaze fixed on the boy's rigid back. Sammarah's head snapped up and her eyes widened in fear as she saw the knife raised above her.

"No, no, " she whimpered. The knife flashed and ripped into the cushion close to her shoulder as she cowered away, falling from the seat. The boy slashed and slashed at the cushion, blind to the fact that his victim had crawled away, then turned and ran amongst the onlookers, shouting and bawling obscenities at them, flailing the knife. They fled indoors, slamming the door, leaving Sammarah huddled in a corner of the terrace and Idral exactly where he had been all along. The boy threw himself in rage at Idral, who grasped him firmly and held him, talking softly, gently, slowly calming him.

As she watched him dealing with the furious child, Sammarah realised that it was not Idral who was weak. Her friend's words came back to her - "Oh no Sammarah, he's not my weakness. He's yours."

CHAPTER 3

" WHAT I COMMAND "

The 'Words'

A)   *"I have said I want to be first in your lives, to be the most important person to you.*
My command is that you have no other god but Me."

B)   *"I have given you My word, the Holy Scriptures, and My Word, My Son Jesus Christ.*
I expect you to obey them both, willingly and lovingly."

C)   *"I command you to keep yourselves holy, to keep your lives free from worldly taints, to live by My statutes, laws and decrees.*
In this way the world will see who I am and will understand My message."

D)   *"I do not want to frighten you or oppress you with harsh, impossible demands, as worldly masters do. I love you.*
I am your Heavenly King and Master, there is no other god but Me."

E)   *"My law is absolute, I made it, I alone, to achieve My purposes, none other, and it is good.*
Walk in it and you will prosper and know peace."

No Other God

Introduction

Exodus 20:1-17

"And God spoke all these words:
"I am the LORD your God, who brought you out of Egypt, out of the land of slavery.
You shall have no other gods before me.
You shall not make for yourself an idol in the form of anything in heaven above or on the earth beneath or in the waters below. You shall not bow down to them or worship them; for I, the LORD your God, am a jealous God, punishing the children for the sin of the fathers to the third and fourth generation of those who hate me, but showing love to a thousand generations of those who love me and keep my commands.
You shall not misuse the name of the LORD your God, for the LORD will not hold anyone guiltless who misuses his name.
Remember the Sabbath day by keeping it holy. Six days you shall labour and do all your work, but the seventh day is a Sabbath to the LORD your God. On it you shall not do any work, neither you, nor your son or daughter, nor your manservant or maidservant, nor your animals, nor the alien within your gates. For in six days the LORD made the heavens and the earth, the sea, and all that is in them, but he rested on the seventh day. Therefore the LORD blessed the Sabbath day and made it holy.
Honour your father and your mother, so that you may live long in the land the LORD your God is giving you.
You shall not murder.
You shall not commit adultery.
You shall not steal.
You shall not give false testimony against your neighbour.
You shall not covet your neighbour's house. You shall not covet your neighbour's wife, or his manservant or maidservant, his ox or donkey, or anything that belongs to your neighbour."

CHAPTER 3   " WHAT I COMMAND "

What is different about this set of *'Words'*, compared to the two previous sets? It is the tone. Up to now it has been powerful but gentle and pleading. Here it changes and becomes strong and authoritative, eliciting respect. Why doesn't God start this way in *Set One*? I suggest it is because He knows us too well. Although He has a sovereign right to lay down the Law, we do not respond well to such an approach and above all else, because of His great love for us, He wants us to respond well, with all our hearts. He wants our relationship with Him to grow and it will only do so in accordance with His rules. Therefore He has to ensure that we engage with His rules. He is wise as well as loving, so He captivates us first, before introducing the necessary issue of obedience to His Law. As Selwyn Hughes observes, "The law does not precede God's grace; it is given to a people already redeemed"

The Psalmist was intensely aware of this. Read right through Psalm 119 for evidence of that fact. From beginning to end it is steeped in references to God's law, statutes, precepts, commandments and so-on, with a happy acceptance of them and a marked willingness to know and obey them more and more. It is this attitude, I believe, that God is seeking from us in response to this third set of *'Words'*.

Note Exodus, 20:1 starts; *"And God spoke all these words:"* not 'God spoke all these commands'. To the Hebrews, a word from God *was* a command, to be followed and obeyed. These *'Words'* are a mixture of command, instruction, encouragement, exhortation and demand. God leaves no avenue unused in His loving pursuit of us, because He is determined to make us His.

God First

" I have said I want to be first in your lives, to be the most important person to you"   'Words' Three A

"I am the LORD your God, who brought you out of Egypt, out of the land of slavery."   Exodus 20:2

In *Set One*, where He introduced this idea, all He said was; *"I want to be the most important person in your lives."* However, now He adds in a little qualifier. *"I want to be **first**"*. We were looking at status in *Set One*. Now we are talking about priority. What priority do you afford God? Is He central to your life, so that He has top priority in all your thinking and acting, or is He peripheral, a useful adjunct on the sidelines? For most of us I guess, the situation is somewhere between the two. He is not satisfied with half and half though. He is not suggesting that it might be a good idea if we gave Him a bit more attention, He is commanding us to put Him first, before anything else we think or say or do.

As He states in Exodus; "I am the LORD your God". I have reproduced the lettering used by the NIV here, indicating that the word being used for God is 'Yahweh', or Jehovah, meaning 'to be actively present'. This is no distant God on the sidelines. This is God, if you'll excuse the expression, mucking in with us, right in the thick of it, repeating His wish to be most important to us and adding to it the rider that therefore we have to make Him first in our lives.

Chapter 3   " What I Command "

The Command

" My command is that you have no other god but Me."   'Words' Three A

"You shall have no other gods before me."   Exodus 20:3

This is getting serious. While God allows us the free will to vacillate, prognosticate and prevaricate to our heart's content if we so wish at the same time, He issues us with an ultimatum: "I want" therefore " I command". His command is to have no other god but Him, which is the outcome of putting Him first, making Him most important.

Military command demands that a soldier serves only the one nation and obeys only the one commander. What a picture of the Christian's obligation. We are enlisted to serve only the one 'nation' - God's heavenly kingdom and to obey only the one commander - the supreme commander of all, Almighty God. He then directs us to obey the legal secular authorities over us, but this does not oblige us to put them before Him.

We can pay lip service to this command, but I think, if we examined our lives, we might find they bear witness to a very different picture and that we actually have a range of things, different for each individual, that take precedence all too frequently over the claims of God in our lives. These can be seen as 'other gods' and we are commanded to have no other gods. They have to be relegated to their proper place in God's order of things, where they cease to be 'gods', or dropped entirely. If we want to fulfil what we were created to be and what our souls and hearts long to be, then we have to have no other god but Him. God first and most important in our lives is theory agreeing with practice, a correct perspective as the result of a proper alignment of our lives.

The given Word

" I have given you My word, the Holy Scriptures, and My Word, My Son Jesus Christ."
                                                          'Words' Three B

"And God spoke all these words:"   Exodus 20:1

One of the greatest gifts of God's grace is His Holy word, the Scriptures. Many households have a Bible. How many people actually open it and read it though? Many years ago a work colleague of mine who attended church faithfully week after week, said to me, in reply to something I had tried to quote by memory from the Bible, "Oh I don't read the Bible," ! Often it's there simply to solve the religious crossword clues, or it was Gran's, therefore it's kept for sentimental reasons. What a travesty of its real purpose. Treating it in this way is a bit like using gold to make the handle of a yard broom. What really puts us to shame when we fail to value the scriptures are the desperate pleas for Bibles from our persecuted brethren who face dire punishment, even death, if they are discovered in possession of a Bible, or so much as part of one.

Is it because it is too readily available to us in the West that we take it for granted? Do we lack hunger for the word of God because we are too full of junk food spooned to us by the media? There is a call here as important as the calls to worship and repentance that we looked at in Chapter 1. It is the call to the word; to the written word, the scriptures and to the spoken Word, our Saviour Jesus Christ. Military personnel muster to the flag. This is our flag. Why are so few mustering?

CHAPTER 3   " WHAT I COMMAND "

Obedience

" I have given you My word, the Holy Scriptures, and My Word, My Son Jesus Christ. I expect you to obey them both, willingly and lovingly."

'Words' Three B

"You shall have .... You shall not make .... You shall not bow down .... You shall not misuse .... Remember .... You shall labour / you shall not do any work .... Honour .... You shall not, you shall not, you shall not, you shall not, you shall not."

Exodus 20:3,4,5,7,8,9,12,13-17

When I was teaching, every September we sat down with our new class to establish the classroom rules. A key guideline was to keep them positive. Lots of 'do this' and 'do that' were held to be more effective than lots of 'Don'ts!'. Look at God's 'classroom rules' here, and I don't use that term lightly, and what do we see? Lots of don'ts, or 'You shall nots' . Contrary to the received wisdom of the educationalists, I found without exception that the childrens' suggestions were more negative than positive because knowing exactly what was not allowed made them feel secure. We also need the security of knowing where the boundaries lie with God, and He provides amply for that need. Our part of the deal is to submit to His rule. Anything other than submission is simply disobedience. This is God's tough love in action. He lays down tough, strong rules for us to follow that will be a safeguard for us.

Furthermore He expects obedience that is willing as well as loving. Willing is a two edged sword. Acting willingly is simply doing whatever is being asked. Being willing however is an attitude, being determined to do a thing. It is the latter that God expects and that it should be done lovingly is only fair when you consider how much He loves us.

Purity

" I command you to keep yourselves holy, to keep yourselves free from worldly taints, to live by My statutes, laws and decrees."   'Words' Three C

"You shall not make for yourself an idol in the form of anything in the heaven above or on the earth beneath or in the waters below. You shall not bow down to them or worship them; for I, the LORD your God, am a jealous God,"
Exodus 20:4-5

I know there is a lot more about purity in the Ten Commandments than just this one dictate. However I want to focus on this one in this section. God has not made it His second Commandment at random. There is nothing more important except His command that we have no other gods. Censure of idolatry is the next logical step. God is demanding that we carry our commitment to Him into every corner of our lives, not just our 'spiritual pigeon hole'. Such purity, such holiness needs continuous maintenance, hence the repetition of the word keep - 'keep yourselves holy'; 'keep your lives free from worldly taints'. Taint is not a common word these days, a quaint expression from a byegone era. Permit me to indulge in a little word - play. As children we used to enjoy the game of removing letters from one word to make another one. Remove the 'a' from taints and you have tints, which expresses beautifully the effect of tainting on our lives. Impurity colours our lives, staining them wrongly and this immediately mars and weakens our witness. I know we can never present a perfect example of Christian living, only Jesus can do that, but that is no excuse for allowing anything less than pure or holy to remain in our lives once we become aware of it.

CHAPTER 3   " WHAT I COMMAND "

Statutes, Laws, Decrees

" I command you to keep yourselves holy, to keep yourselves free from worldly taints, to live by My statutes, laws and decrees."   'Words' Three C

"You shall not misuse the name of the LORD *your God, for the* LORD *will not hold anyone guiltless who misuses his name. Remember the Sabbath day by keeping it holy. .... Honour your father and mother, ... You shall not murder. You shall not commit adultery. You shall not steal. You shall not give false testimony against your neighbour. You shall not covet .... anything that belongs to your neighbour."*   Exodus 20:13-17

I have summarised the commandments here to highlight their breadth and compass as well as to tie them in with the *'Word'* under examination. Misuse of God's holy name is prevalent nowadays and goes unremarked, let alone uncensured. Within the church, let us ensure that under no circumstances whatsoever do we misuse His name. In respect of the world's misuse, let's keep the issue in perspective. Salvation comes first, cleaning up the act follows.

Remembering the Sabbath is an issue full of pitfalls. Suffice to say, God inaugurated a beneficial rhythm to our days on earth and we do well to keep to it, doing an honest, reasonable amount of work and taking sufficient rest. The break is as important a part of the work process as the carrying out of tasks. It is a day for being restored in the Lord, as well as for pleasure.

The first four commands deal with our relationship with the Lord, and rightly precede the rest, which are societal, governing our relationship with each other. Altogether they cover everything necessary for a life free from worldly taints.

Worldly Masters

" I do not want to frighten you or oppress you as worldly masters do, I love you."
'Words' Three D

*"I the L*ORD *your God am a jealous God, punishing the children for the sin of the fathers to the third and fourth generation of those who hate me, but showing love to a thousand generations of those who keep my commandments."*
Exodus 20:5-6

We might tremble with awe when we contemplate the deep things of God, or the awfulness of sin and godlessness; we might weep as we plead for mercy for our unsaved loved ones, our nation or a sinful people. We know there is a judgment for all men to face, but we who are loved by God need have no fear of that. God, in His grace and mercy, gives us deep reassurance and comfort here, when we may be worried that we will fail Him in these demands.

When I do not carry my worries and fears to the Lord, I suffer far more than I need. I have had to learn, and I'm slow to do so, to be open with Him, to freely acknowledge my worries, then to surrender them completely to Him. Only then can He assuage the worry, comfort and support me, so that in turn I can comfort and support others in the same situation, if they will allow me to. We do not receive this kind of care from those over us in the world, no matter how altruistic or humanistic they may be. In many cases they do not even offer minimal help, simply expecting workers to leave their worries behind and get on with the job. Add to this the pressures piled on in the workplace and there is the picture of the oppression of worldly masters. God wants the bright beam of His love to scythe through all that, right into your heart, to lift, encourage, comfort and support you. You only have to let Him do so.

CHAPTER 3   " *What I Command* "

Our Heavenly King and Master

" I am your Heavenly King and Master, there is no other god but Me."
'Words' Three D

"I am the LORD your God, ... you shall have no other gods before me."
Exodus 20:2-3

The similarity here is stunning. Deliberately so I believe. God intends **us** to sit up and take notice, never mind the world! This is really the climax of *Set Three* of the *'Words'*. The following two sentences take us gently down from the heights, ready to move on into the next set. Here God powerfully reminds us of who He is.

All creation is bound up and held in those two little words, 'I am'. Jesus used them too, many many times but specifically in discussion with those who challenged His authority. *" "I tell you the truth," Jesus answered, "before Abraham was born, **I am**!" At this, they picked up stones to stone him, but Jesus hid himself, slipping away from the temple grounds. "* John 8 : 58-59 Jesus' claim was too radical for the authorities of His day to accept, with a few individual exceptions. Why is God at such pains to reiterate His celestial position? I believe the reasons are twofold. Firstly, He is reminding us that He is the Heavenly King of Kings, in possession of all power, of strength beyond anything we could imagine. This should give us complete confidence in Him. Secondly, it is to recall us to a right regard for Him, as Lord of the Universe. In spite of humankind's puny attempts to discredit Him, He remains absolute God. This is God known as 'Adonai', Lord and Master, a name that "contains the thought of ownership, lordship and divine authority." [Selwyn Hughes]. This is Who we follow, Who we depend on, Who we have as our Master. What is there for us to be afraid of? Why run after any other substitute?

NO OTHER GOD

Walking in His Law

"My law is absolute, I made it, I alone, to achieve My purposes, none other, and it is good. Walk in it and you will prosper and know peace."
'Words' Three E

"God spoke all these words :
I am GOD, your GOD, ...
No other gods, only me.
No carved gods ....
No using the name of GOD, your GOD, in curses or silly banter; ....
Observe the Sabbath day, to keep it holy. ....
Honour your father and mother ....
No murder.
No adultery.
No stealing.
No lies about your neighbour.
No lusting after your neighbour's house - ...."   Exodus 20:1-17
'The Message'

The *'Words'* draw our attention to the fact that God made His law for a specific reason - *".... to achieve My purposes, none other, ..."* He intended us to have a lawful framework by which to live and regulate our societies, but in keeping with Divine economy, He also drew up His Law to achieve His purposes for His creation.

The terms Commandments and Law are interchangeable. Laws founded on the Commandments are destined to endure, whatever social upheavals abound around them. Laws founded on man's ideals tend only to last as long as men are prepared to sustain them. If we walk according to God's Law, we will know prosperity and peace. It will not be peace in a worldly sense - 'oh, anything for a quiet life!', nor necessarily will it mean absence of warfare. It is that deep abiding peace of heart in all circumstances, good or bad, that true disciples become ever more acquainted with.

CHAPTER 3   " WHAT I COMMAND "

Story 3)   **The Crusader**

Imagine a scribe, well more a medieval cleric, toiling away at one of those beautiful illustrated manuscripts they produced. It has taken him ten years so far, between other duties, to write and illustrate the first four Psalms, but he is deeply content with his work. Happy in his willing service to his Divine Master. But then war is declared and, as the son of a local nobleman, he is required to leave his churchly occupations and adopt a military persona. Deeply distressed and resentful at having to leave the calm, ordered tranquility of the cloisters he loves he begrudgingly exchanges his clerical garb for a suit of armour over the clothes of a nobleman soldier.

There is little love lost between him and his father. Obligation and duty force our young man to obey his father's summons and he rides away to war with his father and the rest of the fighting men. They endure many fierce battles and as the campaign draws to a final, cataclysmic conclusion, the young man finds himself in the fiercest part of the fighting, shoulder to shoulder alongside his father, out-numbered and out -strengthed by the opposition.

An opportunity arises for the young man to make an escape, a wrong move by one of the enemy briefly opens up a route. In that split second the young man glances at his father to see if he's noticed the chance and realises he's too closely engaged in fighting to be able to escape, without bringing pursuit and capture on them both. Their eyes meet and hold. It seems for a second that the noise of battle recedes and time stands still. Deep within that look is recognition that they both love each other very much. Then the father gives the minimalist of nods, the son slips away safe and free and the father is engulfed and slaughtered by the enemy.

The son wanders for many years in foreign lands after this and has numerous other adventures. Eventually, in middle age, he returns to his father's lands and rides up to his father's castle, where an older brother is now Lord, with his wife and a huge brood of children.

Realising there is no place for him at his old home, our cleric / knight sits wondering where to go. A little girl, one of his brother's children, skips past him, stops, turns and regards him seriously.

"Are you my Uncle Peter?" she quizzes him.

"I am indeed."

"Tell me a story then," she demands, proprietarily settling herself on his lap. He thinks a bit and then tells her about a funny incident he had with a pig that wouldn't be driven to market and ran amok all through the cottage of the old lady who owned it. The little girl enjoyed the story and demanded more. He obliged with several more, until a nursemaid came looking for the child for a meal and bustled her away with much telling off, for disappearing, for wasting the gentleman's time, for getting her clothes dirty and her hair messed and so -on.

Peter watched them go, sadly reflecting that he's got too much time to spare, never mind not wasting his time. Slowly, he gathers himself and his belongings up, fetches his horse and rides off, still with no clear idea of where he is going. Before long he reaches his old Monastery. It is abandoned and falling into disrepair. He recalls all those happy years spent there and goes to see if the Library is still intact. The door is hanging off one hinge and the room is empty. Dust, dirt and debris lie everywhere. Birds nest on the high shelves and other furry creatures have made their homes lower down.

In the centre of the room, lit by a bright shaft of sunlight stabbing down through the broken roof, is the row of high desks where Peter and the other clerics used to work. A long buried memory stabs him painfully. His father is shouting and his mother crying, pleading for something. His brothers are standing to the side, neutral expressions on their faces. Then more comes back to him. He has been discovered stealing apples from a poor cottager, a serf living under his father's protection. His father's rage knows no bounds.

As he relives the scene, he knows what is about to happen. He flinches as the memory of the beating he received floods back. It was more severe than any he had known before, but even worse, were the chilling words of banishment uttered afterwards by his father in a cold, dismissive tone of voice, entirely devoid of any love. It is this that his mother is pleading against. As he leaves the hall, the sickening sound of his father's hand striking her cheek to silence her is the last thing he hears of his home. It stays with him for years until he learns to blank it out. A servant escorted him to the Monastery, where he is to

Chapter 3 " What I Command "

live, a virtual prisoner yet free to go if he had the means to. He grows up there to be a fine young man and learns to be at peace.

Looking at the little row of desks now, he wonders what became of the monks. Then he is filled with a great longing to find his mother's grave, assuming she must be dead by now. He hurries to the churchyard, scouting round for the family graves. It is there. The date of her death inscribed on a block of stone was three days after his banishment from his home.

What veil of tears had followed his departure and her death he can only conjecture. His father had adored her. What had he suffered at losing her so precipitately? He shrugged. He would never know. Bending to murmur his love and say sorry he knew what he'd do now with the rest of his life.

He entered a Monastery, took his vows and in time became an Abbot. He gave many years loving and willing service to God and to the communities where his Monasteries stood, in penance for what he had done to his parents by one, simple, thoughtless, childish misdemeanour. But, oh, those apples were the best! Sweet and juicy, none like them grew in the Castle orchards. His brothers used to pinch them too. They just weren't unfortunate, or careless enough to get caught as he had been.

What sustained him through those last years of his life was the look of love that passed between him and his father that day on the battlefield. From that look he knew that his father had suffered the pain of separation as much as he had. The knowledge that his father's love was still there, after all the years that had passed, comforted and completed him as a person until he died at a ripe old age, contented and full of years.

As with the previous two stories, now you have read this one, stop to consider what thoughts come to mind in relation to the *'Words'* it is written to illustrate?

CHAPTER 4
"WHAT I ORDAIN"

The 'Words'

"I ordain :-

A)   My Church   ....   to reflect My glory in the world.

> ' How little of My glory shines out from your churches. How much of your paltry glory masks My wonderful glory, when you pursue worldly ends instead of heavenly ones.'

B)   My people   ....   to share My love with the world.

> ' Where are the prophets, teachers, evangelists and missionaries for this age?'

C)   My Son   ....   to bring salvation to the world.

> ' Why are you whispering when you should be shouting the Good News?'

D)   My word   ....   to feed the hungry of the world.

> ' Why are you so preoccupied with the social when you should be focused on the spiritual?'

E)   My creation   ....   To satisfy My love.

> ' How is it that I look for the fulfillment of My creation and I do not see it?'

CHAPTER 4   "WHAT I ORDAIN"

Introduction

Joel 2:28-32

"And afterwards, I will pour out my Spirit on all people.
Your sons and daughters will prophesy, your old men will dream dreams, your young men will see visions.
Even on my servants, both men and women, I will pour out my Spirit in those days.
I will show wonders in the heavens and on the earth, blood and fire and billows of smoke.
The sun will be turned to darkness and the moon to blood before the coming of the great and dreadful day of the LORD.
And everyone who calls on the name of the LORD will be saved; for on Mount Zion and in Jerusalem there will be deliverance, as the LORD has said, among the survivors whom the LORD calls."

As with the fourth set of *'Words'*, this Chapter has a slightly different format than the other four. It is divided into three strands :-

Strand 1   *'The church as the people of God'*,
Strand 2   *'Jesus as the Word of God'*
Strand 3   *'The creation as the work of God'*.

These strands tie the passage from Joel with the main thoughts in the *'Words'*. Each Strand is then further divided into *a*, *b* & *c* threads, linked to specific verses from Joel 2. Not only is the format changed, but the way God is expressing Himself has changed. We have already been challenged about His position and status in our lives. Now we are being prompted to allow Him to direct the running of our lives in all aspects.

In the name of clarity, I want to point out that the term 'ordain' does not refer to the ordination of people to the priesthood, through the hierarchy of Bishops, Priests and Deacons, as some people may understand the term. Here it has a far wider application, referring to five specific conditions that God has set-up, by which His creation is ordered and His work is done.

Strand 1   ***The Church as the people of God***

a) Servants

"My people .... to share My love with the world"　　　　　'Words' Four B

"I will pour out my Spirit on all people .... Even on my servants, both men and women, I will pour out my Spirit in those days."　　　　Joel 2:28,29

Although we, the people of God, are living in the last days, the Last Day itself has not yet arrived. Although Christ ushered in the true new age, we are still living in the old fallen world. Therefore the task of the church is to engage fully in mission and evangelism until Christ comes to earth again for the final time. The phrase 'My people' is used here in the sense of *1 Peter 2:9 "a chosen people, a royal priesthood, a holy nation, a people belonging to God "*. We are not talking about mankind in total. We are looking specifically at those who belong to the Christian church.

What is our job description as servants within the 'people of God team'? Simply '.... to reflect My glory in the world, ... [and] to share My love with the world'. We will look at the first requirement in Chapter 10, so all we have to consider here is sharing God's love with the world. This is the companion piece to our direct service to the Lord. It is the horizontal as opposed to the vertical, reaching out as we reach up. Servants work for others, not themselves, although they receive their fair wages. Christian servanthood is not servitude, or slavery. We are free, with status and we are rewarded, spiritually, for our labour. Like the servants in Jesus' parable, let us so labour as to hear our Master commend each one of us; *"Well done, good and faithful servant!"* Matt. 25:23

CHAPTER 4   "WHAT I ORDAIN"

b) Prophets

"Where are the prophets .... for this age?"   'Words' Four B

"Your sons and daughters will prophesy,"   Joel 2:28

Joel gives us a useful role model as a prophet. He looks back, to the Exodus, recalling his readers to the miraculous works of God that have already taken place for their benefit. Then he looks forward, promising miracles to come, building on the hope inspired by what has come to pass. These days we are surrounded by all kinds of gloomy forecasts; wars, global warming, environmental disasters, increasing crime rates, social unrest and so-on. Even the people of God can be depressed and dispirited by such a constant barrage. Prophets of Joel's calibre are needed in every age, but never more than nowadays.

Yet who is prepared to stand up and declare themselves a prophet? Even in church circles, there is a strange reluctance to do this. At a talk I attended recently, the lady hosting the meeting gave the speaker a fulsome introduction before very hesitantly tacking on the suggestion that this lady might be described as, well, a sort of prophetess really. Why such reticence? I think it's to do with a wrong idea about prophets. We tend to see them as cranks or extremists, although once they're dead, we're happy to say they were right all along! But, the Lord is asking 'Where are the **prophets** for this age?' Not, where are the folk prepared to do a bit of prophesying on the side? We are all called to be willing to receive a word from the Lord and share it with the church when necessary. I believe He is looking to raise up individuals right now whose specific Christian calling and service is prophetic. I would challenge you to seek His will in this matter, through devout, listening prayer. Is He calling you to this ministry, or is He prompting you to guide someone else into this vital work of prophecy for this age?

c) Visionaries

"My church .... My people to share My love with the world."
'Words' Four B

"your old men will dream dreams, your young men will see visions."
Joel 2:28

As with prophecy, there are specific individuals selected and gifted by God to receive extra-ordinary pictures, allegories, dreams and suchlike that reveal His purposes in the world. However, as every Christian can receive a prophetic word, so every Christian can be a person of vision. What should our vision be though?

The kind of vision I believe God wants all of us to have is of a different order. We have to catch God's vision of His kingdom, which is the rule of His will on earth. Jesus taught us to pray 'Your will be done, on earth as it is in heaven.' In heaven, God's will is done in every tiny little detail. This is how He wants to see it being done on earth, this is what we should visualise whenever we pray. This vision should underpin our entire lives, as individuals and as a church. That petition from Jesus' prayer is our 'vision statement'. How often do we revisit it, refreshing it in our minds, memories and imaginations? Not frequently enough I would respectfully suggest. Let us commit ourselves to a fresh vision of God's kingdom reigning on earth today as it does in heaven all the time.

CHAPTER 4   " WHAT I ORDAIN "

Strand 2   ***Jesus as the Word of God***

a) Call on His Name

"My Son to bring salvation to the world."   '*Words*' *Four C*

"And everyone who calls on the name of the LORD *will be saved"*

Joel 2:32

This is the message we carry to the world. Call on the name of the Lord and you will be saved. First of all though, do we believe it ourselves? Time for a spiritual health check. If your world is being shaken at this moment, if you are being stirred up because you know that you do not know, love and trust Jesus, have never made a commitment to Him or laid down your life for Him, then this is for you too.

Joel foretells a time when God would pour out His Spirit on all people. Such an outpouring is mentioned in the *'Words'*, *Set One D*, and by inference, in *Set Five B*. Recently we have undoubtedly seen outpourings of the Holy Spirit in certain specific places, with some dramatic results. What I believe the Lord is longing to do now is pour out His Spirit to a degree previously unheard of or imagined, across the entire, worldwide church, rather than in isolated little pockets here and there. When He does, the world, especially 'the world' of the church, will be shaken and we will all need to call on the name of the Lord. Are you ready for that? Are you praying for such a revival? I believe we should all be praying most fervently for God to work in this way. Who can deny that the world is in need of it?

b) Deliverance

"My Son to bring salvation to the world."   'Words' Four C

"for on Mount Zion and in Jerusalem there will be deliverance, as the L*ORD* *has said"*   Joel 2:32

Who or what are the enemies we need to be delivered from? *"You, my brothers, were called to be free. But do not use your freedom to indulge the sinful nature;" Galatians 5:13*. We have been freed from the tyranny of sin by Jesus' victory on the cross but we constantly have to guard against becoming enmeshed in its clutches again. Deliverance is as essential for the Christian as it is for the non-Christian.

Joel spoke truly when he saw the victory of God over his enemies, and His eternal Presence with his people, although of course he had no idea when his prophecies would be fulfilled. Just as we are guided by St Peter to see the Christian significance of Joel's prophecy, so we are also taught in the New Testament to see that in Christ the blessings which Joel predicted are available to all who "call upon the name of the Lord ".

Joel saw the enemy as personified, in the heathen, Gentile hoards attacking Jerusalem and the Jews. There are plenty of hoards attacking the church from without, hostile authorities, the media and so-on, but also a plethora of ills within the church that are undermining its very fabric and heart. Some of these are mentioned in *Set Five* of the *'Words'*, indifference, compromise, materialism, hypocrisy, defeatism. They are symptomatic of so much of the unbiblical thinking that prevails in the church today and they constitute as great a threat to the church's existence as any amount of external pressure or persecution.

c) Survivors

"My Son to bring salvation to the world"   'Words' Four C

"there will be deliverance, as the LORD has said, among the survivors whom the LORD calls."   Joel 2:32

The Biblical idea of the remnant is what Joel means by survivors, but there is more to understand here. The *'Word'* is a simple statement of all that God is doing in His world, for His creatures and throughout history. Salvation is deliverance, through Jesus' redemptive action on the cross. It is not limited to a specific few but is freely available to all who seek it.

Ask yourself, what sort of person is a survivor? What qualities would they need? In the NIV this verse is cross-referenced with *Zechariah 13:8-9* " *"In the whole land," declares the Lord, "two-thirds will be struck down and perish; yet one-third will be left in it."* There is the idea of the remnant of course, but read on. *"This third I will bring into the fire; I will refine them like silver and test them like gold."* This is what is meant by survival. Coming through traumatic, painful, testing times and coming through victoriously.

Zechariah continues *"They will call on my name"*. Note the grammar. Not 'they might' or 'they could' call on the name of the Lord but 'they **will**' call on His name, expressing certainty and confidence. We should make it our habit, to call on the name of the Lord, in order to survive the stresses and strains of life, as God intends us to. We are called to be survivors, not casualties, and just like survivors, we will end up safe and secure - *"I will say, 'They are my people,' and they will say, 'The Lord is our God'."*, He affirms in Zechariah. What more could we ask?

Strand 3   ***The Creation as the work of God***

a) Wonders

"*My creation to satisfy My love.*"   '*Words*' Four E

"*I will show wonders in the heavens and on the earth,*"   Joel 2:30

What can be more wonderful than God's creation? Where I live, I can ascend a nearby hill and take in the glories of His natural creation and the splendours of the view from all compass points. You will undoubtedly have similar places near you. A few months ago my husband and I visited Rosemoor, a garden belonging to the Royal Horticultural Society. The day was damp and cheerless but we proceeded with our visit nevertheless. The drizzle got stronger, but the miracle was, it laid the dust so that everything looked fresh and it enhanced the colours so that they shone with a luminosity you would never see on a dry day. At the time I thought 'this must be a bit like the new heaven and the new earth God has promised us. ' This is the wonder of His creation in its entirety.

There is more though that He wants to show us. The real wonder of His creative activity is the motivation behind it. He is doing it all 'to satisfy My love'. He has ordained the creation to support the human life He has placed within it, in order to ensure His own fulfilment as the God who is love through our response of love for Him. That is awesome. I can scarcely take it in.

CHAPTER 4   " WHAT I ORDAIN "

b) Change

"My creation to satisfy My love."   'Words' Four E

"The sun will be turned to darkness and the moon to blood"   Joel 2:30

Terry Wogan recently had a Deaconess doing the thought for the day slot in his programme on Radio Two. 'How many Anglicans does it take to change a light bulb Terry?" she queried.
"I don't know," answered he, "how many Anglicans does it take to change a light bulb?"
"Change?" she shrieked in a terrified tone of voice. Apologies to all Anglicans.
Being creatures who prefer to maintain equilibrium, we all dislike change. Not only is it foretold throughout the scriptures but we also desperately need change in our hearts and lives, and in the action of the church in the world, in order to comply with God's desire to fulfil His love. The changes I believe God is asking of us are within our control. Joel's signs and wonders belong more to the realm of the allegorical, mythical type of story like Tolkein's 'Lord of the Rings', currently an immensely popular Film. There is a sense in which the sun can be turned to darkness in our lives as well. We will examine this in greater detail in Chapter 10. Let us be heartened, in spite of the shaking up that God's changes will produce, we know He will be there with us all through it.

c) The day of the Lord

"My creation to satisfy My love." *'Words' Four E*

"The sun will be turned to darkness and the moon to blood before the coming of the great and dreadful day of the LORD" Joel 2:31

The phrase 'day of the Lord' refers to the coming time of judgment, when God will finally intervene in the affairs of the nations. Its climax will be the revealing of the new heaven and new earth I referred to previously. It also includes the consummation of God's kingdom, His triumph over his foes and His deliverance of his people.

What therefore has the day of the Lord, the coming day of judgment, got to do with His statement that He ordained His creation to satisfy His love? Judgment does not sound all that loving on the face of it. Thoughts of sheep and goats and being consigned to the outer darkness where there is wailing and gnashing of teeth come to mind rather than thoughts of love. Yet it is a loving God who has ordained the day of judgment.

In fact it is the day of the culmination of all that God has been working towards since He started His work of creation. It is the day when all He intended for His creation can come to fruition and all that mars it can be got rid of completely, for ever. A day when He, and His children and all of heaven, can look on the creation, see it in its fullest glory, working entirely as it was intended to work and see that it is indeed good. The day of the Lord is not a day for the people of God to fear. It is a day to await in breathless, eager anticipation, a day when the love of the God of love is fully satisfied in all particulars and in every way.

Chapter 4   "What I Ordain"

Story 4)   ***Two Churches***

Let us take two churches, side by side on a city street. One a magnificent edifice raised to the glory of God in Victorian times. Tall, dignified, ornamented tastefully. Large stained glass windows and an imposing arched doorway grace the front. Replacement plate glass doors have recently been fitted, to show off the wide entrance lobby, where a table stands, adorned with an eye-catching flower arrangement. Above the table a suitable picture is hung on the freshly painted wall. Large door mats keep the polished oak floor pristine clean, brushing the street dust and dirt from shoes as worshippers gather for services.

The other church is a lowly building, crouching insignificantly in the shadow of the first, to the left as you face them both. It is built of plain old red bricks with a corrugated iron roof and beaten up wooden doors, padlocked against vandals. Small mean windows high up in the walls and a shabby notice board, blue paint faded and peeling, the remains of gold lettering advertising service times, are all the features on the front of this church. Tatty railings surround its front yard. You have to go down three steps and across the yard to reach the front doors.

Next door, the front entrance is reached up an imposing flight of six steps, straight from the pavement. It has a tiny, neatly paved front area, enclosed by a smart, low stone wall. Either side of the steps are two earthenware tubs containing precisely clipped shrubs. In the small church front yard there is a row of bars to secure bikes to and a large, grubby dustbin. To the side is a lopsided gate, closing off the narrow alley between the two churches, down which is the side entrance to the smaller church. On the other side of the large church is the vehicular access drive leading to parking space and the church hall.

The little church has no hall. Everything happens in the one area in that one. Even the place where tea and coffee is made is to the side of this area, behind a classroom type table. The large church has rooms and places for all kinds of different functions and nooks and crannies for other unknown or long forgotten activities. Enough though, of the buildings. The picture is becoming clear.

Let us take a wander down this street late on a Sunday morning. What do we expect to see as we arrive at our two churches? Stereotypically I would expect there to be a lively crowd pouring out of the smaller church. You know why - the church is the people, not the building. The types who go to the smaller church might not have much of this world's goods, but what they lack materially, they more than make up for in spiritual enthusiasm and growth. Whereas next door, the straggling few worshippers are more interested in Mrs Peabody's hat and the Sunday roast than they are in the things of God. As they file out in orderly fashion, they shake hands politely with the Vicar and some less intrepid souls may even murmur 'lovely service Vicar' or 'good sermon, sir' before rushing off to get the lunch, clean the car, mow the lawn or play golf. Well, you'd be wrong. Just as Jesus turned his hearers expectations upside down and inside out in his parables so often, so this story does not proceed along expected lines. Nor is it the exact opposite of the stereotype.

As we arrive at the smaller church, we see the doors are thrown open wide and a little knot of people is standing just outside, heads lowered, backs to the outside world. Not in prayer, but engaged in worried, urgent discussion. Inside two ladies are clearing away the few used mugs. A bored child is draped listlessly over a nearby chair waiting for his mum to finish this task so they can go home and he can go out to play with his mates.

Not many are coming out of the front of the posh place next door. That's not because not many went to the service. It's because they're all packed into the hall at the back which is humming with talk and sharing as they enjoy their after church coffees. Teenagers mill, children run around, leap on laps, crawl under tables and chairs, spill juice and get told off. People spread out into the car park with their coffee. Little groups huddle, arms around or hands on someone as they pray for them. The three Ministers circulate, catching so-and-so for this and such-a-body for that.

This church is busy, so busy. Next door the church seems dead. Neither is impacting on the vast majority of the town's population living only a few yards away. Yet both are deeply committed in financial terms to a joint church venture in Sierra Leone, raising funds to send two teachers, a medical team, and an agricultural expert to a small rural Christian community.

CHAPTER 4   " WHAT I ORDAIN "

The anxious discussion outside the little church is revolving around the fact that there isn't enough money in the kitty this month, again, to meet their side of the financial pledge to this Mission. Any spare cash has had to be used mending vandalised windows and cleaning graffiti off the front walls as well as improving the toilet facilities so that Social Services will continue to use the building during the week as an old people's Day Centre, which provides a valuable source of income for the church.

Pre-occupations next door are, on the surface of it, more spiritual. A lot of good things are going on, an Alpha course, house groups, Youth Group, women's fellowship, a mid week talk from a visiting speaker, an agape meal with another church across town, the coming Harvest Festival service and supper, to which the Guides, Scouts and Brownies are invited. No wonder this church has three ministers. They need them, as well as the voluntary lay ministry, and business staff, also unpaid. It's a model of good church organisation, a real tribute to God. Whereas next door ....well!

What Is To Be Done about that lot next door is often debated, unofficially of course, amongst the members of the big church. The consensus, not exactly expressed in such clear cut terms, but implied and understood, is that really it would be better if next door were closed down. So few, achieving so little. The building could be put to far better use. Well, the land actually. The building's an eyesore, the only thing it's any good for is pulling down.

But, let's close in on that small knot of anxious people next door. Who do we have here? A pastor, a married man - his wife is helping to do the coffees. He's a bank clerk the rest of the week and pastors the little church for free, as his Christian duty and service. He's young, a bit shy socially, but get him onto Biblical subjects and he waxes lyrical and knowledgeable. There are two ladies, both middle-aged housewives, with older children nearly off their hands and part-time cleaning / shop jobs. There's a retired man, a widower with grown-up children and grand-children. Finally there's a young man who lodges with the pastor and his wife, who have no children. This group, plus four or five other individuals who sometimes join them on a Sunday, constitute the entire congregation of this church. But they always offset their inclination to make gloomy prognoses of its decline with firmly cheerful statements. Their optimism is always of the order that 'something will turn up' although they don't know what and they never consider what they may need to do in order to facilitate that 'something'.

Meanwhile the teenage son of one of those two middle-aged ladies, let's call her Sadie, and him Jason, is perennially in trouble, at school and with the police. At the very moment that Sadie is worrying her head over the fate of the far away Sierra Leoneans, Jason is being bundled into a Panda car having been apprehended with two friends, breaking and entering a local factory premises.

The older of the two arresting officers actually feels quite concerned over these youngsters, particularly Jason, whose Mum clearly can't cope with him and who seems to have no visible Dad. It isn't the first time he's pulled Jason in and, although outwardly stern, he's inwardly exasperated that there's so little he seems able to do to steer the youngster onto better paths. There are plenty of 'youth schemes' and clubs and joint police / school initiatives available, but Jason remains aloof and unaffected by any of them. It's a standard case of horses to water.

So Chris, the policeman, finds himself yet again escorting Jason back home from the police station and explaining what's happened to Sadie. Returning from there, he drops into a local newsagent to get a choc bar to cheer himself up, and to have a chat to Rashid, who owns the shop. As they 'put the world to rights' Chris's eye falls on a leaflet lying on the counter, advertising a forthcoming attraction at the town Rec. "More work for us," he grumbles to Rashid, absently slipping the leaflet into his pocket. In fact the date of the attraction comes and passes without him really noticing, it causes so little bother. Then he bumps into Jason again a couple of weeks later, in the precinct. Jason is milling about with some other lads Chris doesn't recognise, but they seem different in dress and attitude to Jason's usual partners in crime. Intrigued Chris strolls over to pass the time of day. A bit sheepishly Jason greets him and introduces the four lads as Rob, Dan, 'Smiffy', and Tod. They all seem nice, normal young men. They're handing out leaflets.

"What's this then?" Chris asks.

Chapter 4 " What I Ordain "

Tod gives him one.

"Have you thought where you're going when this life ends?" he asks.

This throws Chris. "Er, no."

"Well can I suggest you read that. It'll help you decide." says Tod respectfully.

"What is it then?" queries Chris once more.

"Read it and see," says Jason, with a hint of cheeky humour that is strangely unlike the Jason Chris knows.

Chris turns the leaflet over and glances at the illustration on the front. More intrigued than ever, he starts reading. The boys move off handing out more leaflets. Chris pushes his into his pocket and makes off back to the station. He'd found the leaflet oddly disturbing and would prefer to put it straight in the bin. When he goes to his locker to change at the end of his shift, there it still is in his pocket, and, on the top shelf of his locker, is the other leaflet from Rashid's shop. Without stopping to think why, he takes them both home, to his bachelor flat. It's clear they both came from the same source. The event at the Rec. had been a tent evangelical meeting and the second leaflet was penned by the evangelist and his team.

Chris is deeply moved by the call to repent and give your life to Jesus and prays right there at his kitchen table for help to do just that. A picture of Jason's cheeky grin rises in his mind and he goes straight to Jason's house, finding not just Jason there, but also Tod, who talks him through his commitment to Jesus while Sadie looks on open-mouthed.

Before long Sadie has also given her life to Jesus and a small house group are meeting at her house regularly for prayer for the town. She is stunned at the difference in Jason as he, Tod and a regularly changing set of other Christians go out on missionary forays into the town centre and other places, particularly where the teenagers hang out. Saturday nights become their greatest convert gathering time and soon the question arises of which church, or churches, to encourage these converts to join, so that they can be nurtured in their new found faith.

Both of our two churches are considered by Tod and his team and both are found to be largely unsuitable for the needs of new converts. The larger one because of it's preoccupation with activities geared for long-established church members and the worldliness at the core of their operations. The small one because of its feeble ineffectiveness and self-doubt. Other churches through the town received some new converts, if they lived near them or already had contact with them. For the bulk of the new Christians though, no church was found, readily available. So a new church had to be founded. Before this could happen though, disaster struck. Jason's old buddies were up to their mischief again, breaking and entering and this time setting fires. The building they chose was the little church. By the time the fire brigade arrived, it was pretty well razed to the ground.

The pastor stood gazing at it's dripping remains in despair. His wife pulled him away angrily.

"Leave it," she snapped. "We'll leave this place. This is the last straw. We're not wanted here. I hate it. We'll go."

Weakly, he allowed her to have her way and they left, never to be heard of again. The land was sold off, eventually, to a property developer who built old people's flats on it. However, in one of those strange twists of events, the original owner of the property had inherited it from a distant relative with philanthropic leanings and the will had stated that the property was to continue as a Christian church, or, if sold, a percentage of the proceeds were to be used to build a replacement church elsewhere. This same owner was an Uncle of Dan's, who had been following the events in Dan's life, as Dan became a Christian, with great interest. Not a Christian himself yet, Uncle sent for Dan to discuss the building of this replacement church. Jason, Tod and a few others, including Chris, accompanied Dan to this meeting. The result was the founding of a Community Evangelical Church which met at first in Dan's Uncle's large front room. In amongst all this going on, Uncle and his wife had become Christians too.

What a church this was! Stamping feet, loud Hosannas, groaning in prayer, weeping and singing were heard regularly on Sunday mornings and many times in the week. No-one was turned away who came genuinely seeking the Lord and the membership grew and grew at an astounding rate. People in that town were desperate to hear the word of God. They had been spiritually starving and here were people offering them relief for their

Chapter 4 " What I Ordain "

hunger, spiritual food and drink, bread of heaven and living water from Jesus that never ran out and always satisfied. Nowadays, this church is strong and effective, not only in its own town, but in sending missionaries to other towns in the land. It is rich in spirit and in material wealth, both of which it spends liberally in spreading the full Gospel of Jesus Christ. It has a fine new building, paid for by donations from its members as well as the original bequest, which is open and in use for the glory of God 24 hours a day, seven days a week, 52 weeks of the year.

Our larger church looks to this new church, in chastened and deep repentance for its lack of spirituality, for leadership and guidance in presenting the word of God to the world in a new and powerful way. Out of the ashes of worldliness and defeat arose the fire of effectiveness, spreading the wonder and power of the Lord to all it touched in that place.

This is a longer story with more detail perhaps than the previous three. Maybe you need to read it a couple of times to extract its meaning more fully. What are the *'Words'* and this story saying to you about your Christian walk and your church?

CHAPTER 5
"WHAT I HATE"

The 'Words'

A) *"I hate injustice. I am a God of mercy, requiring mercy. You know that I love all mankind, that I have made all people equal. Any oppression or inequality is unjust and offends against My good and perfect law."*

B) *"I hate indifference. Too often you have been indifferent to the sufferings of others, both near to you and far off, but worse, far worse than this is your indifference to Me, to My gifts, to My word and to My Spirit. Warm your hearts, warm your spirits, fan into fire the flames of passionate love for Me, for My Word and for My world."*

C) *"I hate your compromises. My truth is absolute. I have made that clear to you. My word is founded on My truth. If you think you do not know what the truth is, then you need to know My word, to look for the truth, as I have given it to you, in Scripture. It is there, plain for you to see, but you do not look for it. You prefer to use the easy premises of the world, that are based on erroneous thinking. Read, learn, know and live My truth, and it will set you free, free from the tyrannous power of the world."*

D) *"I hate materialism. Take care that you have godly concern for the use of your money and possessions. Where I bless you with worldly wealth, I do it so that you can do more for Me. I do not give it only for your comfort and certainly not to confer superior status on you. I do it to enable you to spread My gospel and to proclaim My love to all the people I bring within your circle of influence, some very close to you, right where you are living, as well as others further away from you."*

E) *"I abhor hypocrisy, the whited sepulchre of religious pride, the sin that has beset and spoiled too much of the work of My church here on earth. I love to receive the praises of My children as they worship Me with hands and arms raised high, but why are so few of you willing to seek My forgiveness on your knees, even flat on your faces, so that I might forgive and raise you up to walk even more upright lives, pleasing and serving Me and fulfilling the deepest desires of your own hearts?"*

F) *"I hate defeatism. My church is the Church triumphant, victorious. I am not dead, Christianity is not dead. I am very much alive and My followers have life, abundant life, and joy, deep wells of joy, bubbling up in their spirits, bubbling up and spilling over, out into the world around them. Spilling out and always being refilled, refilled from the never-ending source that is Me. How can you walk in defeat when I have given you feet to skip lightly in blissful joy through this life and all its troubles? Shake off your feeling of defeat My children. Lift up your heads, lift up your eyes and see My triumph, see My victory and know that we can never, never be defeated. Amen, so be it. As I have spoken so shall it be. Halleluiah!"*

Introduction

Matthew 5 : 1-12   'The Beatitudes'

"Now when he saw the crowds, he went up on a mountainside and sat down. His disciples came to him, and he began to teach them, saying:

> *"Blessed are the poor in spirit, for theirs is the kingdom of heaven.*
> *Blessed are those who mourn, for they will be comforted.*
> *Blessed are the meek, for they will inherit the earth.*
> *Blessed are those who hunger and thirst for righteousness, for they will be filled.*
> *Blessed are the merciful, for they will be shown mercy.*

CHAPTER 5   " WHAT I HATE "

Blessed are the pure in heart, for they will see God.
Blessed are the peacemakers, for they will be called sons of God.
Blessed are those who are persecuted because of their righteousness, for theirs is the kingdom of heaven.
Blessed are you, when people insult you and falsely say all kinds of evil against you because of me. Rejoice and be glad, because great is your reward in heaven, for in the same way they persecuted the prophets who were before you."

If I had been drawing up these *'Words'*, I would have put this one first, to get the nasty bit out of the way quickly before moving on to the nice bits. The Lord however, always knows best, so this set comes last. In fact, it isn't as nasty as you might expect. Although the Lord does not mince His words when there's something He disapproves of, He also offsets this every time with commendation and encouragement. Furthermore, the last *'Word'* of the set provides a fitting climax to the *'Words'* in their entirety.

This set reminds me of the words of the prophet Isaiah - *".... "my thoughts are not your thoughts, neither are your ways my ways," declares the Lord. "As the heavens are higher than the earth, so are my ways higher than your ways and my thoughts higher than your thoughts." "* Isaiah 55:9 However, although Isaiah had to point out the shortcomings of his fellow men, note that only three verses later he declared; *"You will go out in joy and be led forth in peace;" v 12* The situation is not hopeless for us. The lady leading the intercessions in my church a few Sundays ago was led to challenge us and I would like to echo her challenge here :- 'What pre-occupies you? Would God be content with it?'

Being Merciful

"I hate injustice. I am a God of mercy, requiring mercy."   'Words' Five A

"Blessed are the merciful, for they will be shown mercy."   Matthew 5:7

This *'Word'* reminds us of Hosea 6:6 *"For I desire mercy, not sacrifice"*. The word mercy has the sense of right conduct towards one's fellow men and of loyalty to the Lord. Injustice is exactly the opposite. A merciful man empathizes with his neighbour's troubles, and mourns alongside him. As Shakespeare declared through his character Portia in "The Merchant of Venice", God's mercy *".... is an attribute of God himself;*
> *And earthly power doth then show likest God's,*
> *When mercy seasons justice. -*
> *Though justice be thy plea, consider this,*
> *That, in the course of justice, none of us*
> *Should see salvation. We do pray for mercy;*
> *And that same prayer doth teach us all to render*
> *The deeds of mercy. "*

Mercy is a chosen attitude. We cannot excuse lack of mercy by saying 'it's not in my nature', as if we had no control over it. We are not called to be religious experts but humble servants of God. Everyone can be merciful.

Likewise with injustice. Just as God abhors injustice, so must we. In one of the prayers used in the Anglican communion service, the congregation are invited to ask :- "In your mercy forgive what we have been, help us to amend what we are, and direct what we shall be; *that we may **do** justly*, love mercy, and walk humbly with you, our God." In praying this, we are asking for God's help to do precisely the thing He requires of us.

CHAPTER 5   " WHAT I HATE "

Equality

"You know that I love all mankind, that I have made all people equal. Any oppression or inequality is unjust and offends against My good and perfect law."
'Words' Five A

"Blessed are those who hunger and thirst for righteousness, for they will be filled."
Matthew 5:6

God has made all people equal but looking around the world today, in spite of our massive social, material, and medical advancements, we are still pretty primitive in our human rights record. According to a special report prepared by the organisation Gospel for Asia, although "caste discrimination is officially forbidden by the constitution, it remains firmly in place in Indian social life." Dalits [meaning "broken people", long considered lowest of the low] are supposedly given equal opportunities but the new laws "benefit only a small percentage and are seldom enforced. " What can we do about such a situation? Here's one possibility. "Ram Raj [a Dalit leader] .... asked for the continued support and assistance from the Christian community." We can pray as well as give financially and in any other way the Lord shows us. It is not a question of whether we should do anything, but of how much and what we should do.

Blessed are those who hunger and thirst after righteousness, in their own lives but also in order that the Kingdom of God may indeed come on earth and men and women may be made righteous by God's Holy Spirit at work within them. Injustice offends against His *'good and perfect'* law. There is no higher law than God's, no matter how long men may search for something else. Only God's righteousness gives fulfillment of life and soul.

Passion

"I hate indifference. Too often you have been indifferent to the sufferings of others, both near to you and far off, but worse, far worse than this is Your indifference to Me, to My gifts, to My word and to My Spirit. Warm your hearts, warm your spirits, fan into fire the flames of passionate love for Me, for My Word and for My world."   'Words' Five B

"Blessed are those who mourn, for they will be comforted."   Matthew 5: 4

I have heard the Beatitudes described as 'the *attitudes* that ought to *be* in the lives of true Christians.' We are linking this Beatitude with the *'Word'* that urges us on to greater passion in our Christian lives. Mourning is a strong, passionate emotion. How much do we mourn, not only for our own sinfulness, but also because of injustice and the sufferings of our fellow humans? When we face up to our spiritual poverty, we mourn our lost relationship with God, and lament the iniquity that separates us from Him. We all try to avoid sorrow, preferring to seek joy, yet true joy is often the fruit of sorrow.
What do we need to do to become as passionate as God wishes, about His gifts, about His word, the scriptures and about His world? Paul exhorts us to seek the highest gifts; *".... eagerly desire spiritual gifts."* Romans 14:1 We need to open ourselves wide to the outpouring of the Holy Spirit, not just warming our hearts, but setting them on fire for God.

CHAPTER 5   " *WHAT I HATE* "

Wealth

"I hate materialism. Take care that you have godly concern for the use of your money and possessions. Where I bless you with worldly wealth, I do it so that you can do more for Me. I do not give it only for your comfort and certainly not to confer superior status on you. I do it to enable you to spread My gospel and to proclaim My love to all the people I bring within your circle of influence, some very close to you, right where you are living, as well as others further away from you."   *'Words' Five D*

"Blessed are the poor in spirit, for theirs is the kingdom of heaven."
                                                                               Matthew 5:4

I am aware that this Beatitude deals with spiritual poverty. Luke's version says "Blessed are you who are poor." I once heard a preacher speculate as to why we are less familiar with it. He gave as the reason that Luke's is more uncomfortable. It hits us where it hurts most, in our wallets! But this is a *'Word'* for those blessed with wealth. God blesses us materially - **so that** - we can do more for Him, acknowledging our wealth as His, and dedicating it to His service. So should we sell all we have and give to the poor, as Jesus instructed the rich young man, Matthew 19:16-26 ? Maybe, in specific cases this will be required, but my impression is that Jesus taught more about godly use of money and wealth than He did about giving it all away. Admittedly, in the early church, the members did hold all in common, Acts 2:44-45. If this is genuinely what God is demanding of you, then do it. For the rest of us, we need to consider prayerfully how we use our shekels, firstly to spread the Gospel, at home or abroad, and secondly to meet our personal needs. It will not always be easy but can we avoid it because of that?

Other - centredness

"I hate materialism. .... Where I bless you with worldly wealth, ... I do it to enable you to spread My gospel and to proclaim My love to all the people I bring within your circle of influence, some very close to you, right where you are living, as well as others further away from you."   'Words' Five D

"Blessed are the peacemakers, for they will be called sons of God."
Matthew 5:9

Having dealt with the financial aspect of this *'Word'* now we're looking at the love for others that should characterise our lives and make us peacemakers in the fullest sense. Peace-making is very demanding, but it is required of all Christians, in so far as it is possible for them. Everyone can do something to promote peace, within their own families and immediate neighbourhoods. You don't have to be president of the U.N. to be a peacemaker! We share the Gospel of peace in the first place. Those called to be peace-makers in the wider arena are endowed with a generous public spirit. Their path is a way of courage and they need our prayers at all times. Peace-makers earn the right to be called sons of God ; there is no greater privilege than this. They feel that their own interest is promoted in promoting that of others

There is a tension between being other-centred and maintaining a healthy lifestyle, mentally, spiritually and physically. Paul tells us to do *"nothing out of selfish ambition or vain conceit, but in humility consider others better than yourselves. Each of you should look not only to your own interests, but also to the interests of others." Phil 2:3-4.* Note, he does not say disregard your own interests, but put others' interests before your own. Other-centred people are also humble, secure enough within themselves to be able to discount the strident demands of the self in order to put the needs of others first.

CHAPTER 5   *" WHAT I HATE "*

Hypocrisy

"I abhor hypocrisy, the whited sepulchre of religious pride, the sin that has beset and spoiled too much of the work of My church here on earth."
'Words' Five E

"Blessed are the meek, for they will inherit the earth."   Matthew 5: 5

Religious pride can occur in any religion but let me remind you, these *'Words'* are addressed to the Christian church. It is religious pride that breeds resentments between denominations. It is religious pride that too often alienates those who come seeking solace or answers to their questions about faith. Religious pride is an insidious ill that slinks in by the back door of our lives, threatening to make us, not holier, but holier - than - thou. It is religious pride that makes us shout, like the cured leper in Mark 1:45, 'look at ME! I'm cured! Wow! Just look at ME!', rather than 'Look what Jesus has done for me! Look at **Him**!', drawing attention to the power and might of our Lord and Saviour. Without allowing the sin of religious pride to entangle our hearts, we can rest in our certainty that no-one comes to God except through Jesus, because our pride is not in ourselves, but in Him.

Meekness is maintaining a patient attitude in the face of injury. It is not pessimistic stoicism, nor is it being a doormat. Jesus was meek; but He was not weak. He had all authority to challenge anyone who opposed Him yet submitted to the treatment meted out to Him by His captors, even to the extent of allowing them to crucify Him. What I believe we need to do is come before the Lord, asking Him to root out all sinful religious pride and fill us with that wonderful meekness that enabled Jesus to serve the Father so single-mindedly.

Defeatism

"I hate defeatism."   'Words' Five F

"Blessed are the pure in heart, for they will see God."   Matthew 5:8

To see God means to be His friend and favourite and to dwell with Him in His kingdom. Such a position is unassailable. How can anyone dwelling in God's kingdom be defeated? But achieving the required purity of heart takes a lifetime of practice and even then we only work towards it. Defeatism tells me I am a sinner for ever and there is no hope for me. That is a part-lie. I am a sinner, but there is hope for me, thanks be to God! His son died to procure my salvation and His Spirit continues to convict me whenever I drift into sinful ways, so that I can repent and He can remedy the situation.

Defeatism tells us no -one is perfect, so what's the point in trying? Jesus tells us our righteousness has to exceed even that of the greatest religious leaders, in His time the Scribes and Pharisees. We cannot see how we could possibly manage that but His Spirit comes into our lives as Counsellor, empowering us.

"You're blessed when you get your inside world - your mind and heart put right", Matthew 5:8 'The Message'. Defeatism comes from without and affects what is within, even when it appears to emanate from a little inner voice, whispering negative thoughts. If what is deeper within is strong and 'right' though, it can withstand the attacks of defeatism, no matter where they come from. We have to adopt the attitude of staunch faith, hope and belief in God to sustain us in all our troubles. Sometimes this will take a colossal effort of will, but the second we ask for help from God, there He is helping us.

CHAPTER 5   *" WHAT I HATE "*

Persecution

"My church is the Church triumphant, victorious. I am not dead, Christianity is not dead. I am very much alive and My followers have life, abundant life"
'Words' Five F

"Blessed are those who are persecuted because of righteousness, for theirs is the kingdom of heaven."   Matthew 5:10

I want to focus on two adjectives here, triumphant and victorious. Although they both mean the same thing, this tautology has its purpose. There are two sides to victory, the actual occurrence, and the state of victory, of being the winner. In the Christian context the victory is that won by Jesus on the cross. This was an event in history, proved to have happened by archeological and historical evidence. At the same time, it initiated a state of victorious living for all who surrender to Jesus. His servants may have some wobbly moments, they may spend dry times in spiritual deserts, they may experience what has been dubbed 'the dark night of the soul' when faith seems dim and God far away, but they will find that God will prevail in any and every circumstance, in His good time and in His inimitable way.

The Beatitude specifically mentions persecution for righteousness. Some of the stories you hear about our persecuted brethren are truly sickening, yet over and over again they write things like this; "S. faced much opposition from the people of his own village; but in spite of all the persecution, he never turned back or denied Jesus" [Gospel for Asia] They represent victorious living and can teach us about perseverance and faithfulness. In the West our attackers are perhaps more subtle. Still there is no reason to feel defeated. This is a *'Word'* of encouragement for those undergoing any kind of persecution. It is an injustice and God hates it.

Joy

"My followers have life, abundant life, and joy, deep wells of joy, bubbling up in their spirits, bubbling up and spilling over, out into the world around them. Spilling out and always being refilled, refilled from the never - ending source that is Me."   *'Words' Five F*

"Blessed are you when people insult you, persecute you and falsely say all kinds of evil against you because of me. Rejoice and be glad, because great is your reward in heaven, for in the same way they persecuted the prophets who were before you."   Matthew 5:11-12

This part of Set Five F reads rather like a poem :-

"My followers have life, abundant life,
                              and joy, deep wells of joy,
Bubbling up in their spirits, bubbling up
                  and spilling over, out into the world around them.
Spilling out and always being refilled,
                          refilled from the never - ending source
                                      That is Me."

I've deliberately staggered it in a pattern that enhances the message of those words. Lines one, three and five make a glorious statement about Christian life. Lines two, four and six form a point, spearing into the other three lines, just as joy spears into the life of the believer as they learn to trust God more and more. Finally, there is the climax in line seven, 'That is Me', a powerful assertion. I purposely added a capital letter to the word 'that' . That is Who we know, believe in and trust, none other than Almighty God, maker of heaven and earth and all that is in them, Saviour of our souls and the greatest Lover we could ever have. There will come mockers and scoffers who will revile us for our beliefs, and persecute us. Sadly, sometimes they will be

CHAPTER 5   "WHAT I HATE"

among the people who we would think should love and care for us most, even friends or family. Jesus knew the searing pain of betrayal by a close friend and the sorrow of opposition from a family that not only did not recognise Him for what He was, but also tried to turn Him from His way, thinking they were protecting Him from making a big mistake. How He must have agonised over their lack of understanding and insight.

It is faith that gives assurance and strength to those being persecuted right now, keeping them going persistently wherever God has posted them. Let us give the last word in this Chapter to one of them: -

"At 24, Mahad was already a wanted man. In just eight months, he had led dozens to Christ and planted a vibrant church. With 60 to 70 believers, the fellowship was on fire for outreach and an inspiration to other churches. Despite earlier threats by the anti-Christians, Mahad had not backed down. Now they intended to teach him a lesson and began beating him and his brother.

"While this was going on in the light of the full moon," writes a GFA field correspondent, "suddenly it was totally dark and the attackers became confused and disoriented." The two then broke free and escaped to a nearby jungle where they spent the night exposed to wild animals and a rainstorm. The next day they arrived safely at a GFA home Bible school.

Still determined, the anti-Christians scoured area villages to find the young evangelist, this time intending to kill him. After being bitten by a snake, however, the group leader became seriously ill. And when another attacker came down with an unexplainable, infected sore on one hand, the search was off. "The people in the area were in a state of fear as these incidents became known," the report continues. As a result, village leaders have assured Mahad that he could continue his Gospel work without harassment."

[Yohannan] You see, with God there is only triumph, never defeat. It may be a long time coming and it may have a high cost, but He will never fail to deliver His victories.

Story 5)   **The Six Trees**

In a park there were six trees. The Oak had been there the longest. Its broad sturdy boughs had survived generation after generation of youngsters scrambling up and swinging off. It had lost a few branches in great winter storms over the centuries, but faithfully, year after year it stood firm, providing shelter and habitat for uncountable thousands of minibeasts, birds and small mammals. It was there when the park was part of the estate of a great house. It avoided being bulldozed when a new road cut a swathe across one corner of the estate. As the nearby town encroached and more and more bits of land were sold off by the estate's final owners the Oak tree remained in its little corner, tucked away and untouched. Eventually the Big House itself was demolished and the site redeveloped as offices. All that was left of the great estate was an awkward quarter acre plot containing the Oak tree.

The town council bought but did nothing with the plot for many years, money being thought better used for other schemes. Children still played there, illicitly, not the privileged offspring of the mansion's owners any more but children from nearby housing estates. For them, the Oak still offered its strong branches unstintingly to climb and swing on.

Towering above the Oak, with a long thin trunk and a little bottle brush of branches and greenery at the very top was the Pine tree. The children didn't bother with this one so much. Its trunk was scratchy and had no good footholds for climbing and the branches were too far aloft to get amongst and build tree houses in, like they did in the Oak tree. The best thing about the lone Pine was its fir cones which they eagerly gathered to add to collections or to use in their games. The squirrels were about the only creatures to use it regularly and a few birds nested high in the top.

The Silver Birch was a bit of an interloper. A weed really. A bit of scrubland had been left spare by the builders of an adjacent batch of modern houses. This little plot had been annexed by the council and tacked onto the main quarter acre. Several Silver Birches, self-setters, had taken root there but some were vandalised and others did not prosper. This one was the sole survivor. Although spindly and weak looking, it was actually quite well

CHAPTER 5 "WHAT I HATE"

established. Too flimsy for climbing or swinging from and without enough foliage to provide deep shade on hot days, it was really only decorative, with its pretty peeling silvery bark and new bright green leaves in Spring. The children liked to use its twiglets for their play, as swords or guns. On a breezy day it made a pleasant swishing sound which they pretended was the sea.

At the furthest extreme from the Oak was the Beech tree. It was the last remnant of a beautiful avenue of Beeches that had led to the Big House. It stood tall, proud and stately. This tree had witnessed the passing of carriages to and fro carrying the residents of the house about their business, bringing visitors in all seasons and thronging guests to Summer Balls, Spring Weddings, Christmas Parties, family funerals and state occasions. It had seen the wealthy and famous pass up and down the avenue, right into the twentieth century and the advent of the combustion engine, when the carriages were gradually replaced by expensive, luxury motor cars. Then it had witnessed the rapid decline of the family fortunes and the inevitable dissipation of the estate. The immaculately maintained driveway beneath its branches had been wrenched up by a JCB, all its companion trees felled and now even the grass around its roots, once kept neatly trimmed had been left to grow lank and unruly. It stood alongside an access road for one of the new housing areas. The children didn't bother with it much, except to circle it on their bikes, scooters or roller blades, in sharp contrast to the smart little girls and boys who had learned to ride their ponies up and down the avenue beneath the Beech trees in years gone past.

Strictly, the Poplar wasn't in the park at all. It was at the bottom of a long triangular garden of a new house that backed onto the park. It had been planted by the young couple when they first moved into this, their first home and they were keen to make it something to be proud of. They knew nothing about gardening and even less about trees! They had seen the little Poplar at the Garden Centre and had liked its elegant, contained shape, thinking it would be exactly right for the furthest corner, complimenting the little waterfall and statuary next to the house. They were somewhat perturbed as it began to grow far taller than they had anticipated or wanted. In the winter storms they were dreadfully afraid it would come crashing down onto their newly added conservatory. It did whip and lash alarmingly but it stayed in place, its success in this due to the very fact that it did give and bend to the force of the wind rather than attempting to resist and remain rigid.

Even so, the wife regarded it with a nervous eye, especially when she put her first baby out in his pram to take the air. She worried her husband so much about it that he took the advice of a tree surgeon. Two sturdy lumber jack lookalikes arrived the next week in a beaten up truck, with ropes and chain saws and lopped the top off the Poplar. Now it looked silly rather than shapely, but at least it was safer. The years rolled on and the young couple moved away, selling the house to a retired man and his new wife, who were not interested in gardening, preferring foreign holidays and sophisticated town based amusements. They offered the council the bottom end of the garden, for a sensible price and they purchased it, so that now the cropped Poplar officially grew within the area designated for the park.

At the same time, against the fourth side of the parkland was a smallholding and scrubby 'horses field', long fallen into disuse as the owner became elderly and incapacitated. He was found one day, dead in his armchair, having probably been thus for several days before anyone discovered him. Probate failed to unearth any relatives to inherit the damp, cold house that had been his hermitage for years. The fields were rented from the council anyway, for a peppercorn rent that was years in arrears. So these too were added to the Park scheme and debate ranged hotly over how to make best use of all this land. Two decent sized football pitches could be made out of the smallholding section and the town's football club quickly took advantage of this. For the rest of the park, the council ran a competition for design ideas and canvassed various television companies to see if a garden make-over programme could be made about the park. None expressed any interest, it was too big, too expensive or too ambitious for them. So the hotchpotch of plots that constituted the park lay fallow and unsightly a little longer.

Then several seemingly unconnected events occurred simultaneously, as they do. A lady who was registered blind was voted onto the council, the nephew of a well known T. V. gardening personality moved into a house near the park and a group of silly-billy 14 year olds got themselves into trouble and gave

Chapter 5 "What I Hate"

themselves a scare when they accidentally set light to some bushes in the middle of the park area one hot summer's night. There were letters in the paper saying the area was a disgrace and calling for 'something to be done', a petition was sent to the council, the curate of the local church started up a prayer group to pray for all the town's youngsters, who had nowhere safe to hang out and another worthy lady from the same church started a conservation society which both the blind councillor and the T. V. person's nephew joined, as well as some of the 14 year olds. After a few meetings in which they looked at slides of estuary reserves in foreign climes or heard long boring talks from ecologists working up remote mountains or at the Poles, the conservation society decided its time would be far better spent seeing what needed conserving locally. The park was the most obvious candidate for their attention. The two entries for the design competition were retrieved from someone's In - tray and discarded as hopelessly impractical. The only clear notion they had came from the blind lady, who said it should be a place that had stimuli for all the senses and full access for anyone who was handicapped in any way. They all agreed on this.

Then the T. V. person's nephew suggested he contact his Auntie. She was currently in the middle of a series of programmes devoted to exactly such community projects. He was sure she would at least come and look at it, even if she rejected it. She turned up two weeks later, looked at the plots, considered the draft ideas of the conservation society, went back and looked more closely at the plots then went away. After an interminably long fortnight she came back to them with an innovative idea of her own, calling it the 'Five Senses Experience Park', using scent, colour, texture and sound to create five distinct sections, each one focusing on one sense while incorporating elements of the others and simultaneously containing features that would echo the land use from other times, when some of the land was the great estate and some the smallholding. She, or more accurately her researchers, had done their homework thoroughly. It appeared that, in his day, the smallholder had been something of a character and very much at the centre of town life. To cover the fifth sense, taste, and to commemorate him, she had drawn up plans for an elaborate recreation of a walled Victorian kitchen garden, complete with species and varieties of fruit and vegetables that were falling into extinction and the produce of which could be sold either to help pay for the upkeep of the park or to raise money for charity.

It was a masterful plan. All it required was a large body of willing volunteers to carry it through, under the direction of a steering committee chaired by the nephew and advised by the T. V. expert. Many months hard toil lay ahead of them, with plenty of difficulties to overcome, not the least of which was actually finding enough helpers. Here the 14 year olds came into their own, badgering, bullying and coercing friends, family, neighbours and any other town's person they could into joining this happy band of conservators. Work started in the Spring and all went as well as could be expected with minor hitches and set backs, to say nothing of the wonderful British summer weather, wet, wet and more wet!

The Oak tree took pride of place in the children's adventure playground, alongside a wooden climbing construction, with a wobbly rope bridge, slides, tunnels and towers. A tyre swing was firmly attached to a lower branch and a strongly made tree hideout fixed a bit further up, reached by a well secured but cleverly hidden ladder. The Pine tree was pressed into service as one support for the climbing frame. The Silver Birch naturally took its place within the multi-sensory nature of the park, and two more were planted in triangular formation to create a glade with seating in. The magnificent Beech stood at the new entrance to the park, the grass being cut and attended to around its base and bulbs planted there for early spring colour. Beside it were erected two specially commissioned wrought iron gates with the family crest of the original estate owners in the centre of one and the town's coat of arms in the centre of the other.

The Poplar was a bit of a problem, being lopped, so the initial plan was to fell it and replace it with something more suitable, as it was right where the T. V. lady wanted an attractive vista at the end of a walk. This part of the project got shelved temporarily because other parts kept needing urgent attention, so for now the Poplar stayed put.

Finally, all the attention of the volunteers and the T. V. crew turned on the last bit of the park to be dealt with. This was a large patch in the middle of the old

Chapter 5 "What I Hate"

'horses field', banked up to house height and covered with a further twenty or thirty foot growth of gorse, holly, hawthorn and willow, as well as every weed known to British gardeners, including rampant brambles and bindweed. A JCB and a dumper truck were brought in to clear this space, alongside the more hardy volunteers wielding pickaxes, long-handled shears, choppers and so-on. They attacked it on all fronts, fast and furiously, until someone yelled 'Stop! Stop! Look!' The manual workers downed tools and waved madly to stop the machine operators before turning to see what all the fuss was about. Right in the centre of the thicket, in a wide hollow depression stood a magnificent tree that had been obscured, all but the topmost branches, from outside by the prolific growth up the banks surrounding it.

"Oh wow! Awesome!" breathed one of the teenagers. "What is it?"

"A tree, you plonker!" replied another teenager as everyone fell about laughing, the spell broken.

"Actually, it's Aesculus hippocastanum," declared a knowledgeable gentleman volunteer.

"Horse Chestnut to you," explained the T. V. lady.

"It's HUGE!" said the girl, wide eyed.

"Great at conker time!" piped up a younger volunteer.

"Why's it down in here?" someone wanted to know. "With these banks built up all round it. Strange!"

Nobody had the answer. Theories abounded and the knowledgeable gent was dispatched to conduct a research survey to see what could be dredged up about the tree. They set to once again, even more keen now to clear the surroundings. Two days later the tree stood alone, revealed in full glory. Easily 20 metres tall, it was a text book shape and richly covered in distinctive palmate leaves. Beneath its widely spreading branches was a huge circular area of welcome shade from hot sun or shelter from sudden downpour.

This tree completely eclipsed the fountains that had been intended as the central feature of the park, rising victorious and triumphant over the mess that had reigned so long at its roots and that had threatened to defeat the volunteers when they came to attack this last bit of desolation, their numbers depleted by the falling off of the less stalwart, fair weather friends of the project, and their spirits depressed at the tough challenge this last bastion had thrown them.

A speedy reassessment of the focus of the paths and walkways soon showed that it would be a simple matter to put this specimen tree at a pivotal point in the pattern, with paths leading to it from 5 compass points and giving vistas of it from each angle. Because of this, the problem with the little Poplar, at the end of a side vista fell into place easily. It no longer mattered. The little tree was trimmed to a pointed lozenge shape and a bower built under it out of trellis, across which two clematis were trained, the whole creating a pleasing living sculpture. The direction of the path leading to the Poplar was altered to go past it and on towards the main player in the drama, the Horse Chestnut. With this last bit of the work accomplished, the jigsaw was complete and the park was ready for its grand opening day. A barbeque and a buffet, tea, coffee and squash were all laid on. The Mayor had his robes and chain on, the Vicar wore his best surplice, the T. V. lady actually had clean hands and mud - free jeans and everyone else was attired as they thought fit for such an auspicious occasion. Under a heavenly blue sky the cameras rolled, the speeches were made, the scissors produced and the tape cut. Applause rang out, and continued to ring out after hands had stopped coming together as a summer storm burst upon them all. Everyone dashed for the Horse Chestnut tree and waited, dry and comfortable, beneath its shelter until the storm passed and the jollifications could begin. At the end of the day, everyone declared it a success and the town had a lovely park, presided over by the Horse Chestnut tree, to enjoy for years and years to come.

It is appropriate that this story, coming at this point in the book, should point ahead to good things to come. Before going on to the remaining ten chapters just pause again and ask yourself what relevance this story has in the light of *Set Five* of the *'Words'* and what it teaches us about our personal lives and our churches.

CHAPTER 6

" PATTERNS IN THE 'WORDS' "

Introduction

This chapter looks at five patterns, one for each set of *'Words'*, which constitute very powerful visual images. They were revealed to me by the Spirit as I continued to meditate on the *'Words'*. The patterns for the first three sets are fairly straightforward. The pattern for *Set Five*, however, eluded me for a long time and it wasn't until I had got it right that I realised that my thoughts about the pattern for *Set Four* were also wrong. I was attempting to draw out a castle battlement, which is a vivid image that does provide a helpful insight. Castle battlements were built to withstand assault. God's battlements, all that He has ordained, can be depended on to withstand every assault no matter how fierce. Even so I was not one hundred percent confident about this pattern so I left it and when I returned to it, the image of the stairway became crystal clear.

Working out the patterns drew me ever deeper into the structure underlying the *'Words'*. This structure carries import and enhances the meaning and implications of the *'Words'*. It is not random, nor is it simply artistic or decorative. The fact that there is such a carefully wrought structure to these *'Words'* bears further witness to their true Author, our precious Heavenly Father.

Even if you normally find diagrams confusing or are not helped by pictorial representations, please do not leave this Chapter out. Ask the Holy Spirit to aid you in making sense of the diagrams and to illuminate them to you and I add my prayer that you will find them as exciting and instructive as I did. The Chapter also forms a useful link between the straightforward commentary of Chapters 1 to 5 and the more reflective interpretations of the next four chapters, another good reason not to skip over it.

1) **The Arch**

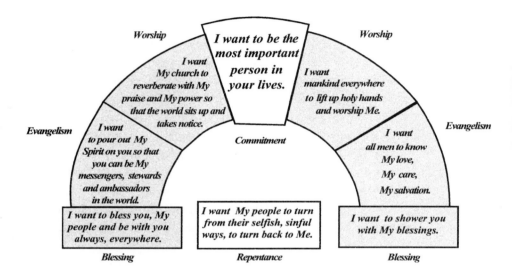

'Words' Set One   'What I want'

CHAPTER 6   "PATTERNS IN THE 'WORDS'"

This pattern is one that St Paul used often, if you examine the passage from 1 Timothy 2, you will find that he has used it there. It has a posh name, derived from the Greek I understand. It is a Chiasmic arch [pronounced Kiasmic] which is "a pattern in which the writer makes a point, then makes two or more other points .... Idea A, Idea B, Idea C, Idea D, then backpedals through the points in reverse order: Idea D, Idea C, Idea B, Idea A. .... in all chiasms, the second half is a mirror image of the first half." [Cunningham & Hamilton] We can compare the chiasm to an arch, "with the centrepiece forming the keystone of the argument" [Ibid.] The words of *Set One* form exactly such an arch, the keystone of the whole thing rightly being God's statement **"I want to be the most important person in your lives."** From this statement flow not only the rest of the ideas in this first set of *'Words'*, but also the thoughts of all the other sets.

Across the base are the foundation stones of blessing and repentance. Down the two sides, mirroring each other, are God's thoughts concerning two key aspects of the church's work, worship and evangelism. Whichever way we read the arch, we cannot avoid the call to repentance, which both precedes and follows blessing, giving more power to our elbow in evangelistic efforts, drawing more people into commitment to and worship of God, to go out and start the whole process over again.

In any arch, as the engineers will know, there are stresses and each part of the structure supports the others. Without any part, the arch will be weakened and may become unable to bear weight which would be critical if it was a bridge, or worse still, it may even collapse, which could be disastrous. So it is with this process. We cannot take shortcuts. God is relying on us to form the bridge over which He can come to the world with His message of salvation. Shall we be strong, each stone in its place, or weak, with missing links all over the place?

2) The Pyramids

> **D ii)** Above all else I desire you with all My heart and long for you to desire Me with all your heart.

> **C ii)** I am deeply hurt when you are indifferent to My love and careless of My affection.
>
> **D i)** I long for you to reject all your other lovers and to remember your first love for Me, so that I can gather you close into My arms and whisper My endearments to you.

> **B ii)** I long to adorn you with the adornments of My love, with gifts and garments, graces and a new name known only to Me.
>
> **C i)** I am an aggressive lover, pursuing you, My beloved children across the plains of Earth and Heaven, seeking to save, redeem, protect and nurture you.

> **A i)** I desire a romantic relationship with each one of you.
>
> **A ii)** I long to be as intimate with you as the very air you breathe.
>
> **B i)** I rejoice over you with singing, My delight is in you and you are desirable to Me.

'Words' Set Two   'What I desire'

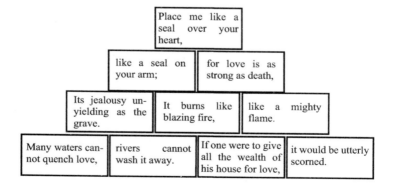

Song of Songs 8:6-7

CHAPTER 6   " *PATTERNS IN THE 'WORDS'* "

This is a similar structure to the Arch, in that it has an identifiable 'keystone' and a definite left / right symmetry. The keystone here contains the climactic appeal of *Set Two 'Words'*; ***"Above all else I desire you with all My heart and long for you to desire Me with all your heart."*** The Bible passage from Song of Songs also conforms to the shape, the difference being, it only reads from the top down whereas the one from the *'Words'* can be read either way. During an in-service training day when I was teaching we spent some time evaluating our school reading scheme. The advisor running the day selected a book from an early stage of the scheme, at random, and read it out loud to us, from the back to the front. It made exactly the same sense as if he had read it correctly from front to back! The point he was making was that it was such bland, pedestrian stuff that it didn't matter which way you read it. If you look at the pattern in the *'Word'*, what is being demonstrated for us here is the nature of our communication with God. When all channels are open, it flows up and down unimpeded, crossing and intertwining. Although you can read it up or down and it still makes perfect sense, it cannot in any way be said to be bland, pedestrian or uninteresting. This and the passage from the Song are in fact full of the most exciting message anyone could ever hear.

Now, as we know pyramids served two purposes. One, they were burial chambers, useful for tidy disposal of the bodies of dead people, with all the belongings they might need in the 'after life'. Secondly they pointed to the heavens, or the stars, reminding the living of where they believed they were heading after death. We are doubly more fortunate, because as Christians we have the assurance that we are not just going to a vague heavenly place in the stars. We are going to God's heaven, which is a real place, to dwell with Him in never ending joy for all eternity.

3) **The Pavement**

> A i) I have said I want to be first in your lives, to be the most important Person to you.

> A ii) My command is that you have no other god but Me.

> B i) I have given you My word, the Holy Scriptures, and My Word, My Son Jesus Christ.

> B ii) I expect you to obey them both, willingly and lovingly.

> C i) I command you to keep yourselves holy, to keep your lives free from worldly taints, to live by My statutes, laws and decrees.

> C ii) In this way the world will see who I am and will understand My message.

> D i) I do not want to frighten you or oppress you with harsh, impossible demands, as worldly masters do. I love you.

> D ii) I am your Heavenly King and Master, there is no other god but Me.

> E i) My law is absolute, I made it, I alone, to achieve My purposes, none other, and it is good.

> E ii) Walk in it and you will prosper and know peace.

'Words' Set Three   *'What I command'*

CHAPTER 6   " *PATTERNS IN THE 'WORDS'* "

'Words' Sets One and *Two* show us how to relate to God. Once we have established that we can start to move, and how! Not that we have to be perfect before we can work with God, but once we are committed He uses us, powerfully. The pattern for this set of *'Words'* symbolises a pathway, or pavement. It reminds me of the dead straight, paved Roman roads that are still in evidence today. I can almost hear the marching feet steadily progressing from place to place, bringing the benefits of the mighty Roman Empire, although admittedly there was a down side to domination from Rome!

As you can see, this pattern is staggered or offset. The Christian walk, or march, is not always straightforward, direct from A to B without any diversions. The pilgrim is beset with difficulties and doubts, often wavers and frequently doubles back. Hence the pavement is not a simple checked layout, but is chequered, as in 'a chequered, or varied, career'.

Isaiah uses the picture of a highway of holiness, :-

"And a highway will be there; it will be called the Way of Holiness.
The unclean will not journey on it; it will be for those that walk in that Way; wicked fools will not go about on it.
No lion will be there, nor will any ferocious beast get up upon it; they will not be found there.
But only the redeemed will walk there, and the ransomed of the Lord will return.
They will enter Zion with singing; everlasting joy will crown their heads.
Gladness and joy will overtake them, and sorrow and sighing will flee away."

Isaiah 35:8-10

Imagine the children of God, ransomed and redeemed, as they enter the celestial Zion, singing, wearing their crowns of joy, skipping in gladness. This is what we are destined for, Praise be to God! **'*My law is absolute, ...* *Walk in it and you will prosper and know peace.*"**

4) The Stairway

My creation - to satisfy My love.

"How is it that I look for the fulfillment of My creation and I do not see it?"

My word - to feed the hungry of the world.

"Why are you so preoccupied with the social when you should be focused on the spiritual?"

My Son - to bring My Salvation to the world.

"Why are you whispering when you should be shouting the Good News?"

My people - to share My love with the world.

"Where are the prophets, teachers, evangelists and missionaries for this age?"

My church - to reflect My glory in the world.

"How little of My glory shines out from your churches. How much of your paltry glory masks My wonderful glory when you pursue worldly ends instead of heavenly ones."

'Words' Set Four   'What I ordain'

CHAPTER 6   " PATTERNS IN THE 'WORDS' "

This pattern neatly incorporates elements of the previous three. It builds to a powerful climax at the top, but here it is coupled with a challenging question *"How is it that I look for the fulfillment of My creation and I do not see it?"* It has building blocks, reminiscent of the Pyramid, on which are inscribed God's purposes for each of the five specific areas identified. The church, *'to reflect My glory **in** the world'*; His people, *'to share My love **with** the world'*; His Son, *'to bring salvation **to** the world'*; His word, *'to feed the hungry **of** the world'* and the creation, *'to satisfy My love'*. Note the four prepositions that I've put in bold. The church is in the world. That could just as well have said 'reflect My glory around' rather than 'in', but 'in' implies a deeper involvement, followed up by the directive to share God's love 'with' the world. We have to get right alongside our fellow humans, bringing the uplifting dimension of God's love and care into the situation. Then something more comes 'to' the world, salvation from Jesus and lastly God's word, to feed the hungry 'of' the world.

When I was working on these diagrams I found, among the material for a Geography project I taught years ago, a photo of an old ruined monastery with a lovely arched doorway in one wall. There is a flight of steps under the arch, leading you up and through the doorway. 'Steps taking you into God's kingdom' I thought to myself as I looked at it and related it to this book. The stairway pattern in this fourth set of *'Words'* does indeed take you into God's kingdom. Not just through their obvious progress to the final statement concerning the creation, but also through an understanding of the system that God has ordained for His world. It is a regimen that rests securely on the four stout pillars of His church, His people, His Son and His word. We are reminded of Jesus' words to Peter *".... you are Peter, and on this rock I will build my church, and the gates of Hades will not overcome it."* Matthew 16:18.

5) **The Hill**

A) "I hate injustice."

I am a God of mercy, requiring mercy. You know that I love all mankind, that I have made all people equal. Any oppression or inequality is unjust and offends against My good and perfect law.

B) "I hate indifference."

Too often you have been indifferent to the sufferings of others, both near to you and far off but worse, far worse than this is your indifference to Me, to My gifts, to My word and to My Spirit. Warm your hearts, warm your spirits, fan into fire the flames of passionate love for Me, for My Word and for My world.

C) "I hate your compromises."

My truth is absolute. I have made that clear to you. My word is founded on My Truth. If you do not know what the truth is, then you need to know My word, to look for the truth, as I have given it to you, in scripture. It is there, plain for you to see, but you do not look for it. You prefer to use the easy premises of the world, that are based on erroneous thinking. Read, learn, know and live My truth and it will set you free, free from the tyrannous power of the world.

D) "I hate materialism.

Take care that you have godly concern for the use of your money and possessions. Where I bless you with worldly wealth, I do it so that you can do more for Me. I do not give it only for your comfort and certainly not to confer superior status on you. I do it to enable you to spread My gospel and to proclaim My love to all the people I bring within your circle of influence, some very close to you, right where you are living as well as others further away from you.

E) "I abhor hypocrisy ....

... the whited sepulchre of religious pride, the sin that has spoiled too much of the work of My church here on earth. I love to receive the praises of My children as they worship Me with hands and arms raised high but why are so few of you willing to seek My forgiveness on your knees, even flat on your faces, so that I might forgive and raise you up to walk even more upright lives, pleasing and serving Me and fulfilling the deepest desires of your own hearts?

F) I hate defeatism.

My church is The Church triumphant, victorious. I am not dead, Christianity is not dead. I am very much alive and My followers have life, abundant life, and joy, deep wells of joy, bubbling up in their spirits, bubbling up and spilling over, out into the world around them. Spilling out and always being refilled, refilled from the never-ending source that is Me. How can you walk in defeat when I have given you feet to skip in blissful joy through this world and all its troubles? Shake off your feeling of defeat My children. Lift up your heads, lift up your eyes and see My triumph, see My victory and know that we can never, never be defeated. Amen. So be it. As I have spoken so shall it be. Hallelujah!

'Words' Set Five   *'What I hate'*

CHAPTER 6   "PATTERNS IN THE 'WORDS'"

The statements in *Set Five* each contain a pair of opposites. In ***A*** injustice, linked to inequality is set against justice and mercy. In ***B*** indifference to God is sharply contrasted with warm passion for the things of God. ***C*** starkly reveals the difference between God's truth and worldly compromises, while ***D*** presents us with two alternatives for the deployment of our wealth, selfishly for ourselves or generously in God's work. Hypocrisy, the sin of religious pride, ***E***, has as its opposite repentance, leading to God's wonderful forgiveness and finally of course the two themes of defeat and triumph are held in powerful tension in ***F***. As with everything else in these sets of *'Words'* none of this is accidental.

When I asked Richard to give me a hand with the drawing of these diagrams, it just so happened that he had a day free when normally he would have been teaching. We sat down in my new study, in front of my computer for some serious prayer and work on these patterns. When we reached my sketch for this one, a deep frown creased his brow. "What on earth's this?" he queried. I know I'll never get any stars for drawing, but I didn't think I was that bad! We tinkered about for an hour or so, then he had to pop out on a little errand, leaving me to complete a grid he had set up which he was sure would sort out the problem. I typed in all the text, then sat back to look at the effect. Something prompted me to put a guideline down the centre of the page and arrange all the text boxes along this central axis. At that stage Richard returned demanding coffee, as they do. We brought our coffee back up to my study and he regarded my efforts with interest, saying nothing. Then he drew a curved line over the top, a straight line down through the middle, with a cross bar at the top and sat back giving me a triumphant little smile, still saying nothing. Simultaneously I realised it was a hill, and the words "There is a green hill far away" sprang into my mind. So the Hill pattern was born, or revealed, well over two years after the *'Word'* was first given to me. Why did God leave it so long to show me this last pattern? Was it because I wasn't ready or wasn't paying attention? Or was it to do with His timing? Probably a combination of both. Now, however, we have the benefit of pattern to help us get to grips with this very difficult and challenging set of *'Words'*.

This is where those contrasts I talked about earlier come into their own. Going down the left hand side we could put the negative aspects, injustice, inequality, oppression, offence, followed by indifference to God's love, so reminiscent of *Set Two* of the *'Words'*. Further down are three different but equally horrible failings, compromise with the world, materialism and hypocrisy. To say they have historically always beset the church does not condone them. We should ask ourselves why these three are singled out here for special attention? I suggest it is because they are the three most significant failings of the church right now. They are however, dragging us ever further down the slippery slope, into a position of defeat, far from our true position on top of the hill as a beacon to the rest of the world. In the film of Tolkein's wonderful trilogy, "Lord of the Rings" the action ranges from the mountain tops to the very deepest depths imaginable and on many levels in between. Little Frodo Baggins, the hero Hobbit may be fearful at times but never once does he turn back from his quest. Resolutely he presses on. Every time he tumbles down, literally or metaphorically to the bottom of a hill or mountain, he picks himself up and goes on towards his goal. Here, in the last *'Word'* of all, we find the motivation and the strength to pick ourselves up and to start the long climb back to the top of the hill. Our way takes us up the right hand side, where we find encouragement in God's victories, forgiveness and fulfillment in renewed service to Him, as well as power and ability to carry out the work He has assigned for us. There is freedom in our knowledge and understanding of the reality of God, we are released into passionate love for God, for His word and for His world and finally we arrive where we started from, to know the place for the first time, as T. S. Eliot so powerfully observed.

Don't you find it amazing, as I do, that from a section headed so negatively *'What I hate'* God could bring forth such incredible hope and positive encouragement? There is so little condemnation. Only for the things that we know should not be present in our Christian lives and churches. If we put them right, God rewards us with riches beyond our wildest imaginings. Oh wow! Awesome!

CHAPTER 7

" WHO? .... OUR GOD "

Introduction

"In this way the world will see who I am and will understand My message."
'Words' Three C

We turn now to a group of four Chapters, each headed by a challenging question; *'Who?'*, *'What?'*, *'Why?'* and *'How?'*. God is pinpointing some details He wants us to pay particular attention to. Accompanying each question is a short extract from the *'Words'*. In this and the next Chapter it is a single statement. In Chapters 9 and 10 it is a series of quotes.

For this Chapter, the selected statement comes from *Set Three* of the *'Words'*. I intend to dissect it carefully and thoughtfully phrase by phrase so that we gain the full measure of the teaching it contains.

When I was a student, I took a course in Dramatic Art and learned about 'throwaway lines', seemingly insignificant little parts in a play that carried an entire theme or one of the main tenets of the play. You tossed them out with the rest of your lines, hence the term 'throwaway line'. This is one such line. What it is telling us is very, very important. This chapter is about three people or groups; first, God Himself, who He is and what He's like; second the world; and third us, the church. We are being asked to examine and re-focus our thinking about God, examine and realign our relationship with Him and examine and renew our commitment to Him and to the world. The *'Words'* present us with a particular challenge, that we should have no other God and we have to understand the implication of this. It is no mistake that the statement we are going to examine comes at the very centre of the *'Words'*. All that preceded it led up to it, all that follows it flows out of it.

'In this way'

This little phrase refers to everything God has demanded of us in the '*Words*' so far. It encompasses our commitment to Him and our behaviour, lifestyles and attitudes. Because of the way we live we signal to others around us what it means to be a Christian. It is the way of obedience, of following Jesus, and it brings specific beneficial consequences. It is not an easy way, don't imagine I think it is, but we are not left to struggle alone. The key to the enterprise is relationship. In my meditations on this God gave me these thoughts :-

> "This is the quality of the relationship I want - deep, trusting, responsive, exclusive, holy, obedient. Only in such a relationship am I fulfilled and is My purpose fulfilled in creation."

True believers are required to give of themselves in total surrender. This is what Jesus meant when He commanded :- '*Love the Lord your God with all your heart and with all your soul and with all your mind and with all your strength.*' Mark 12:30

Such commitment often runs counter to everything we're led to believe by our upbringing, education and society. Deeper than that, it conflicts radically with our natural human ego. Yet God demands no less. So how do we do it? Thanks be to God, the instant we make a move towards Him, He rushes to our aid, because He is closer to us than we realise and because this is what He longs for more than anything. Before I became a Christian, I had no doubt that God existed and that we went to church out of duty to Him. Nobody ever preached anything about having a relationship with Him though. Consequently it was an entirely alien concept to me. I still remember the sense of relief as I gave my life to Jesus for the first time. As the years have gone by I have fallen more and more in love with my God. As the Beloved says, in 'Song of Songs' - '*My lover is mine and I am his*' .... '*His left arm is under my head and his right arm embraces me.*' 2:16 & 8:3

I'm not always as faithful as I should be and I still struggle, like Paul did, with my selfish, sinful nature. We're all in that boat, but we are all also still beloved of God, as He makes abundantly clear in the '*Words*', Set Two and it is '*in this way'*, as His beloved children, that we should live.

CHAPTER 7 " WHO ? .... OUR GOD "

'the world will see'

'The world'. What do we mean by this, who does it signify? I take it to mean secular society, the non-Christians around us, the 'others' of *Set Five B*. It does not refer to the physical planet, although there is mention of stewardship in *Set One* which implies a right Christian regard for the use and conservation of natural resources. It is a collective noun, for the people who constitute the world, but it is also a singular noun. For 'the world' in that sense, read territory that is not claimed for God from the grip of the enemy.

The world can observe the quality of our relationship with God and this is what God is telling us here. *'In this way the world will see ....'* For the world to see, of course, it has to be looking. Most of the time it is not. The British education system is currently regulated by a body known as OFSTED. One headmaster declared that their inspections were like an out-of-focus snapshot taken with the camera pointing the wrong way! This describes the position of the world vis a vis Christianity admirably! The world, largely, is looking the other way. Why? Could it be because there just isn't anything going on in many Christian churches that is eye-catching enough? I believe that is what God is saying here. We need to put in some deep, fervent prayer for revival to come to the church.

In passing, a personal thought about mission fields. We might need to re-align our ideas on this one. Mission is a core activity of the church, to which the lion's share of its energies and resources should be dedicated. Mission fields are no longer exclusively abroad however. They are right on our very own doorsteps, wherever God has arranged for us to live, although we must still pray and do everything within our means for those in far off lands. There will always be people who are called to go abroad from their home country for the purposes of mission, but this is happening less and less. The important thing is our attitude towards those non-believing neighbours and work colleagues who reside or work in our mission field. How much do we care about them, about their salvation, their eternal destiny? To God, it is as great a concern as His concern for us, His children.

'who I am'

This is the kernel of the statement. We are being asked to sharpen our focus, to renew our concept of this God we serve. I recently attended a dinner at which the speaker was Ian McCormack, a gentleman from New Zealand whose testimony was amazing. Briefly, he had died in hospital having been stung by Box Jellyfish, one of the deadliest poisonous creatures known to man. Although not a Christian prior to this, he was taken up to heaven, right to the very feet of God. His description of God was awesome. Although He is close to us and longs to be closer than the very air we breathe, He is also Very God of Very God. In the *'Words'*, He reveals Himself as a provider, with unlimited resources, as a lover who gives an entirely new substance to the word romantic, as the supreme authority, as the creator, and as a pure and holy God, like no other God. I cannot think of anything He has told us about Himself that is not encapsulated by these five descriptions. This affirmation of who He is stands at the very centre of these *'Words'*. It's where He belongs. In the centre, of my heart and life, of your heart and life, and in the centre of His church. It is to the establishment of His reign of love and law at the centre of His creation that all He does is dedicated.

In the *'Words'* He says of Himself :-

"***I am an aggressive lover,*** " *Set Two C*
"***I am deeply hurt*** *when you are indifferent to My love ....*" *Set Two C*
"***I am your Heavenly King and Master,***" *Set Three D*
"***I am a God of mercy,*** *requiring mercy."* *Set Five A*
"*I am not dead, ...* ***I am very much alive***" *Set Five F*

What a God we have! He is not tyrannous, harsh, or capricious, although He is jealous as we have seen, intolerant of sin and He does convict us when necessary. He is not indulgent, spoiling us when we pester Him for our own way. Yet He is instantly generous when we ask for things within His will. He is most certainly not worn-out or dead, as some would have us believe. He is the same today as He was when the world began and He will be the same when the world ends - Majestic, Powerful, Wonderful, Almighty, Creator God, challenging, dynamic and above all, gloriously alive.

CHAPTER 7   " WHO ? .... OUR GOD "

'and will understand'

Because of what we are and what we do, the world will see who God is and will understand about Him. Well, that's the theory. If the world cast an eye at your church, would that be the case? I pray that you could say yes, but I have a sinking feeling that an awful lot of people would have to say no. Today a card dropped through my letter box from a local church, inviting people to take a Bible Correspondence course. 'If the Bible is a closed book to you ....' it said, before going on to encourage people to attend the course. To so many people, not just the Bible, but the church as well, is a 'closed book'.

I was reading in the UCB daily notes this morning about teaching your children. I haven't made a terribly good job with my own. I did read the Bible to them when they were little, and answered their many queries as honestly and clearly as I could, but neither of them have become Christians, yet! Although one has stated it is all rubbish, I still pray for them. The implication of the UCB notes is that only personal example will draw your children to Jesus. "Try teaching them something *you're* not committed to! Your words will ricochet back in your face. .... they watch you like a hawk. Since your actions say that what you're trying to teach them isn't important to you, it'll never be important to them either. .... When your lifestyle demonstrates a real love for Christ, He'll attract your child like nothing else on earth!" [Gass &Gass] . Allowing for free will, this is true and it applies as much to the church and the world as it does to parents and their children.

When the lifestyle of the church demonstrates the importance of Jesus to each member, then others will be drawn in like iron filings to a magnet. Didn't He say *"I, when I am lifted up from the earth, will draw all men to myself."*? John 12:32 I know John goes on to say *"He said this to show the kind of death he was going to die"*, but Jesus' words have a far wider application than that. He intended His followers to raise His profile high in their communities, to be shining beacons, pointing the way to God for the world. We should still be carrying the torch for Jesus, showing the way so that the world will not only see God, but will understand what God is all about and what they need to do in response.

'My message'

The key thing here is that it is God's message, not ours. We do not own it, nor do we have to write it, He already has. There is no copyright on it, it is in the public domain. Anyone can share it, declare it or use it. Why are we reticent then about spreading the gospel? Why don't I go downstairs right now and tell the man who is mending my leaky roof about salvation in Jesus? I can find all sorts of excuses but no good reasons. I have an Uncle who wouldn't hesitate. At eighty years of age last year, he stood up in the Pub where we were having the 'wake' after the funeral of his sister-in-law, my Aunt, and witnessed to how good the Lord had been to him all his life and encouraged all my cousins and their children who were there, to give their lives to the Lord Jesus Christ, as he had as a young man in his twenties. My cousin from Australia looked across at me and said "Wow! You've got to admire the old boy haven't you? I wish I had his faith." I'd like to say I then witnessed to him, but something else distracted me and the moment passed. I knew though that he was deeply touched by Uncle's testimony.

Earlier I mentioned Ian McCormack, fondly known as the 'Jellyfish man'! A friend had urged me to go with his wife and hear him. She also brought her daughter, her mother-in-law and a lady she works with. My own daughter accompanied us too, with a college friend, because they had heard enough about the 'Jellyfish man' to alert their curiosity. To say we were all enthralled by his testimony is an understatement. None of the party actually went up to the front afterwards, to show they had given their lives to Jesus, but the point I am making with these two stories is that I don't know what was going on in my cousin's heart at the funeral, or in the hearts of our party of guests at Ian's talk. God does though, and it was His message that was proclaimed on both occasions. Does He not say *".... so is my word that goes out from my mouth: it will not return to me empty, but will accomplish what I desire and achieve the purpose for which I sent it." Isaiah 55:11*? When we are faithful and careless of our own comfort or embarrassment, then God will work through us, in many ways, some most unexpected or unusual, to deliver His message wherever hearts are receptive.

CHAPTER 8
"WHAT? .... THE TRUTH"

Introduction

"If you think you do not know what the truth is, then you need to know My word, to look for the truth, as I have given it to you, in Scripture."
'Words' Five C

Examining this extract in the context of the whole of *Set Five C* we see a sharp contrast between truth and compromise. The *'Word'* begins - *"I hate your compromises. My truth is absolute."* There can be no blurring of the truth for the Christian. God has made it plain, it does conflict with worldly thinking and we may not query that or try and blend the two into some sort of mishmash.

You will also notice that compromise is the only one of the six things God tells us He hates to be preceded by *'your'*. That makes our responsibility clear. We *'prefer to use the easy premises of the world'*, denying the absoluteness of God's word, because they are easier. In his book "The Templars", Piers Paul Read says of the earliest Christians that although a few chose the path of compromise, by paying minimal homage at Zeus' altar, the overwhelming majority of believers refused to corrupt their faith or their witness for Jesus, and consequently suffered the most horrible of deaths. In the Western church, we are like the people addressed in Hebrews *"In your struggle against sin, you have not yet resisted to the point of shedding your blood."* Heb. 12:4 I wonder what future historians would write about us? We justify our compromises in many ways - 'everyone's doing it'; or 'well, the Bible's no longer appropriate to the society we live in!'; or 'our's is a multi-cultural society, we must be tolerant'. We do live in a multi-cultural society but we need to replace tolerant with respect, and what we should respect is everyone's God-given right to choose what they will believe. We can also love and pray for all people who follow other religions, but we must not let it be thought that we believe any other religion could lead people to God. Too much woolly thinking predominates in the church today. As an example, I have heard Islam, Judaism and Christianity linked together as the three, equal, Abrahamic faiths, that all lead to God, although Islam denies the Godhead and authority of Christ! I have read so-called Christian books that promulgate the idea that all religions are pathways to God. Jesus declared that *"no-one comes to the Father except through me." John 14:6* and this has not changed. We are God's redeemed children, bought at the inestimable cost of the precious blood of Christ shed for us on the cross. To compromise what we believe in and stand for is exactly what St Paul warned us about - *"Do not conform any longer to the pattern of this world", Romans 12:2.*

We cannot worship the 'version' of God presented by any other religion, without compromising our own faith. People are being led astray and this is the most dire consequence of compromise. Can you honestly say it is alright to do something when you know it runs counter to God's expressed will and may risk not only your own, but other people's eternal destiny? The effect of compromise, in creating false ideas in people's minds, in tarnishing the purity of God's word, in minimizing God's sovereign right to judge all wrong, cannot be under-stated. In fact, if you consider the other five things God hates that are pinpointed in *Set Five*, they could all arise out of compromise. We must take every avenue available to us to avoid compromise at all costs.

CHAPTER 8   " WHAT ? .... THE TRUTH "

'If you think you do not know'

"So I will always remind you of these things, even though you know them and are firmly established in the truth you now have." 2 Peter 1:12. Where would we be without Peter and his humanness? While I admire St Paul, especially as a writer, and respect St John for his powerful intellect and integrity, I can relate to Peter as sister to brother and that is immensely comforting. He had weaknesses and was not afraid to let them show, neither was he permanently inhibited by the consequences of his mistakes. He got up, dusted himself down and started all over again, several times. It takes a strong confidence to be able to do that. Peter had self-confidence, but that is too prone to letting us down when it really matters, which makes it unreliable. The confidence that led to him becoming an Apostle and a founder of the Christian church, that enabled him to preach that amazing sermon at Pentecost was confidence in and from the Lord. It is confidence of this kind that the Lord is exhorting us to have here.

We tend to confuse ourselves. All we need to know is made quite plain by God, yet we still say we do not know what to do or think. We allow our doubts to reign over us. Now don't get me wrong here. It's O. K. to have doubts, we all have them from time to time. It's what we do about them that is crucial. Publicly expressing doubt about the tenets of the faith in the national press, when you are a senior representative of the church, is not O. K. The safest of all places is in your prayer time with God or in private fellowship with a trusted Christian brother or sister. Admit your doubts openly before God and face them in the confident expectation that He will assuage them.

Paul said, *"I am not ashamed, because I know whom I have believed,"* 2 Tim *1:12* We can say, 'I am confident because I know whom I have believed'. When we rely on God, and are fully open to the guidance of the Holy Spirit in our thinking, we need have no fear and we most certainly do not need to compromise with the world or anyone else, for any reason. I will leave the final word in this section with John *".... you have an anointing from the Holy One, and all of you know the truth."* 1 John 2:20

'what the truth is'

This phrase gives the chapter its title, although 'what' here is not a question. Using my favourite device of looking for patterns, I find that there is one for *Set Five C* that we have already seen in the *'Words'*. Check the diagram opposite and you will see it is like a piece of paving. There is a very solid spiritual foundation beneath our feet for us to take our stand on and it is the truth as found in God's word.

There are thirty two things prefixed by the word *'My'* throughout the *'Words'*, the one occurring most frequently being *'My word'*, which comes seven times. Put *'My word'* with *'My truth'*, mentioned three times, and that totals ten, more even than *'My love'*, which has six mentions. This tells us just how important is this matter of the truth. Without a proper understanding of God's truth, and an acceptance of the truth behind His activity in the world and of His miraculous interventions into the events of history, the life and witness of the church is meaningless. Paul knew that when he declared we would deserve the greatest pity of all men if there was no resurrection and our hope was only for this life, 1 Cor. 15:12-19. All kinds of attempts are being made these days, within the church, to discredit God's miraculous acts. Why can't the very people for whom all this was ordained by God, accept the miracles and mysteries as part of His wonderful provision for us? The disciple, the true follower of Jesus who is more concerned for his eternal destiny than for his earthly comfort, will be at ease with mystery, will be able to trust God enough to put it in His hands, accept what He has told us as the truth and live in the light of it.

This is very, very important. Anything that the church does or says, or that its representatives say or do, that runs counter to God's revealed truth or throws doubt on it does untold damage to the church and to society. It cannot of course, alter the facts in any way, or detract from the truth. The truth is as unchanging as the God who made it is unchanging. The church and then the world are the losers when the truth is compromised.

CHAPTER 8   " WHAT ? .... THE TRUTH "

The truth pavement

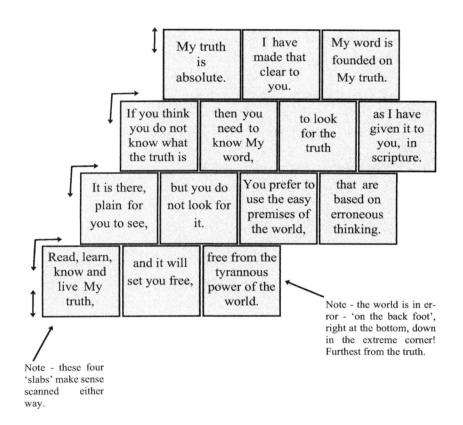

Note - the world is in error - 'on the back foot', right at the bottom, down in the extreme corner! Furthest from the truth.

Note - these four 'slabs' make sense scanned either way.

What is the truth of the situation?

115

'you need to know My word'

If we are unsure of our grounding, or we don't know what to do or say in a situation, here is the answer. We need to know His word. God gave it to us with the intention that we should use it to the full. I like Alex Buchanan's story about his wife's muesli. " She says, 'I can tell you that there are lovely nuts in this muesli, as well as millet flakes, raisins, wheat germ and oats. I can tell you that it will do you good: it will give you energy and maintain your health. But it will do you no good until you get a spoon and eat it!' " Ezekiel was told *"Eat this scroll."* [God's word] *Ezekiel 3:1* and he found it was sweeter than honey and that it strengthened him for the work he had to do for the Lord.

Reading a passage of scripture daily and studying it, either by yourself or within a group of other Christians is a good way to get to know the Bible, but to get the most out of it you need to meditate on it. This is what Ezekiel was being commanded to do, figuratively, when the Lord commanded him to eat the scroll. "Meditation .... is the digestive system of the soul" says Selwyn Hughes, likening it to the process of rumination by which animals such as cows or sheep chew the cud, extracting every last gramme of nutrition from it. It isn't difficult, but it does require discipline. There are lots of books on Biblical meditation on the market and I recommend that you get one and get started, either on your own or preferably, in a small group of other Christians. Make sure it is Biblical meditation though, which will bring you closer to God and is totally safe as it is under His control.

Brother Yun strongly advocates learning the Bible by heart. The students at his training school were "required to read through the entire New Testament and memorize a chapter a day. One month after the start of the class most of the students could quote the whole Gospel of Matthew by memory." What an asset, when their Bibles might be seized at any time, or they might be thrown into jail and deprived of them. We do not have this urgency in the West, but the discipline in itself has much to recommend it

CHAPTER 8   " WHAT ? .... THE TRUTH "

'to look for the truth'

Let's be sure about this - God's truth is not affected by any trends in philosophy, society, politics and so-on, as some people strangely seem to believe. It is complete as it stands. We are taught that our lives should bear the marks of holiness and righteousness. This is not easy, nor automatic, but for every failure in this area there is always a means of reparation, firstly with God, then with our neighbour whenever it is possible or appropriate. We may have to eat a bit of humble pie, but rather that than leave a wrong unrighted, which mars our relationship with God and others, and destroys our peace. You may be familiar with the idea of 'keeping short accounts with God', not allowing anything wrong to linger in your life, but dealing with it promptly and truthfully before God. Like the psalmist, we need regularly to invite God to; *"Search me, O God, and know my heart; test me and know my anxious thoughts. See if there is any offensive way in me, and lead me in the way everlasting"* Psalm 139:23-24.

God urges us; *'look for the truth, as I have given to you, in Scripture. It is there, plain for you to see but you do not look for it'*. I've highlighted that little sequence deliberately. **'Look - see - look'.** God is stressing the importance of all this. *'Read, learn, know and live My truth and it will set you free.'* We are all familiar with the idea of freedom as expressed by Jesus in the Gospels, but how many of us are still caught up in our inhibitions, especially about openly witnessing to our faith? Are these inhibitions due to our lack of knowledge of God's word, undermining our confidence, or do we prefer to express worldly ideas in order to get along easily with non-Christians ? Knowing His word is the only way to take a stand against ungodly ideologies, temptation, insidious influences and the beguiling premises of the world. Without the truth woven deep into the underlying canvas of our lives, the picture we portray to the people of the world will be indistinguishable from their own life patterns and will offer them nothing as an incentive to find out more about God for themselves. Surely our greatest wish for all those we love or care about, is that they should come to know their Saviour?

'as I have given it to you, in Scripture'

God tells us that His truth is *'given'* to us, is *'made'* and *'revealed'* by Him, and that it is *'good'*, *'plain'* and *'available'*. Nothing very startling about any of those. Perhaps that's why the people who challenge God's truths think they are right to do so; maybe they feel that is too simplistic for so profound a concept, but in effect, they are holding the truth in contempt.

God puts it simply, simply so that we will follow it. God's truth is, however, the deepest, most complex mystery we will ever encounter. We can never plumb its depths nor understand every aspect of its intricacy. It is woven into the very fabric of existence, it governs all God's dealings with His creation and it drives the laws on which the universe is founded and operates. Every discovery mankind makes about the universe only serves to show him more about God, if he has the eyes to see this.

There is a very close link between God's truth and His law. The same statement is made about both of them. *'My truth is absolute'* is a clear echo of the earlier statement in Set Three D *'My law is absolute'*. Where do we go to seek God's law? We go to His word of course, the Bible, which He has told us is founded on His truth. Is there any other source? Not that I know of. Events, under the controlling hand of God, can influence a decision or outcome, even negatively, but always for the ultimate good of all concerned. I couldn't count the number of times I've needed to know what God's will is for me. For every one of them though, the answer or the guidance has always been biblical.

If you look at the diagram opposite, you will see that there is a stepped shape to the left hand side as there was on the Truth pavement. There are also some arrows beside the pattern, but they are unlike those beside the Truth pavement, which go upwards as well as downwards making sense whichever way they are read. When I drew the Law pavement in rough and added the arrows, I annotated the sketch with the comment 'one way only, no two ways about it!' In God's law, in God's truth and in God's word, there are no two ways about it. He made them and He intended them to work in His way, for His world, throughout all time.

CHAPTER 8   " WHAT ? .... THE TRUTH "

The Law pavement

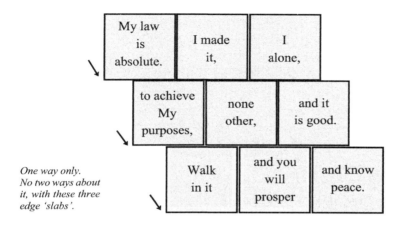

One way only. No two ways about it, with these three edge 'slabs'.

What is the law for?

CHAPTER 9
" WHY? .... FOR THE SAKE OF - "

Introduction

1) *"Why are you whispering when you should be shouting the Good News?"*
'Words' Four C

2) *"Why are you so preoccupied with the social when you should be focused on the spiritual?"*   'Words' Four D

3) *" .... why are so few of you willing to seek My forgiveness on your knees, even flat on your faces, so that I might forgive and raise you up to walk even more upright lives, pleasing and serving Me and fulfilling the deepest desires of your own hearts?"*   'Words' Five E

These three parts from the *'Words'* are particularly challenging. They make it very clear why we should have no other God. It is not only for our own eternal salvation. It is also for the sake of the world, because we are called by God to reach the world for Him. The Christian church is the only religious body to have knowledge of the truth of eternal life, a knowledge granted to us by Jesus Himself. It is not God's intention that it should stop with us though. It is His intention that we should freely share that knowledge, in His strength and with His help.

I also believe He has given us these *'Words'* just now for three reasons. First and foremost, for His own sake, to fulfil His love. Second, for the sake of the world and the church, to save as many lost souls as possible, and third for the sake of every individual Christian, that we might become the holy, righteous people He longs for us to be, dwelling in close intimacy with Him. We serve a wonderful God who not only commands us, but also loves us and therefore enables us to do what He commands. In partnership with Him, and filled by His precious Holy Spirit we have all we need not just to carry out our task reasonably well, but to complete it fully and triumphantly.

Whispering v shouting

"Why are you whispering when you should be shouting the Good News?"
'Words' Four C

Before we consider the implications of this question, I want to ask another. What should be whispered? There is a clue, earlier on in the *'Words'* :-
"I long [to] **whisper My endearments to you.** *" Set Two, D*
Many people are familiar with His still, small voice speaking in their souls. Non-Christians think we're barmy when we talk about it and consider fetching the men in white coats to take us away. They have some justification, murderers and serial rapists have blamed their actions on their 'voices'. Let us never confuse the voice of God speaking to the believer with this other manifestation which is from the evil one. How do you know the difference? This is a spiritual phenomenon and it is spiritually discerned. Test it through prayer, laying it open to the Spirit. Then wait for the assurance of deep inner peace and confirmation through scripture. Sharing it with a trusted spirit-filled Christian friend for them to concur is also good. Don't forget either that just as He whispers His endearments to us, so we can also whisper our endearments to Him.
So what should be shouted, not whispered? The Gospel, of course! Bad news seems to prevail, holding us in its thrall while good news passes by almost unnoticed. We do not shout the Good News for a multitude of reasons. First there's embarrassment. Then there's doubt, or there's self-preservation, something people living under repressive regimes will be more familiar with. The wider you open yourself up to His love, as God pleads with you to do, then truly, the more that perfect love will drive out these negative feelings. You may be a little nervous, but believe me, if you approach others in a state of surrender to God's love for you and for them, then doors will open for you to share the message. In the love and power of God then, let us not be afraid to declare our faith, if not literally at the tops of our voices from the rooftops, at least clearly and unequivocally and in as many ways as we can to capture the attention and interest of as many people as possible.

CHAPTER 9   " WHY ? .... FOR THE SAKE OF - "

Social v spiritual

"Why are you so preoccupied with the social when you should be focused on the spiritual?"   *'Words' Four D*

In my understanding of this question, social does not mean having a good time together, which is quite acceptable to the Lord, as part of living in community. By social in this context is meant social work, or relief in disasters and aid to the poor. Someone has said that the church is the only institution that exists for the benefit of its non-members. Apart from the church's ministry in such areas as discipling or teaching, which are primarily for the benefit of the members, I would say that this is true. We are His provision for reaching the world with the Gospel, although there have been occasions when He has reached people directly and not through the church.

The church is certainly active in the world, some churches are a lot more active than others, but have all the activities got the right priority? K. P. Yohannan, of Gospel for Asia, maintains that the battle "against hunger and poverty is really a spiritual battle, not a physical or social one ...." and that ".... The only weapon that will ever effectively win the war against disease, hunger, injustice and poverty .... is the Gospel of Jesus Christ. To look into the sad eyes of a hungry child or see the wasted life of a drug addict is to see only the evidence of Satan's hold on this world. .... When God changes the heart and spirit, the physical changes also. If you want to meet the needs of the poor in this world, there is no better place to start than by preaching the Gospel. It has done more to lift the downtrodden, the hungry and the needy than all the social programmes ever imagined. .... Social concern is a natural fruit of the Gospel. But to put it first is to put the cart before the horse." "

It is time for the church to take up its true colours again, to refocus its priorities firmly on its first purpose which is to spread the Gospel. There is nothing in the *'Words'* to revoke James' instruction to show our faith by our deeds, James 2:14-26. What we are being called to do, is to give priority to evangelism without abandoning good deeds.

Repentance

> *".... why are so few of you willing to seek My forgiveness on your knees, even flat on your faces, ?"*   'Words' Five E

The Lord is not referring to physical posture alone here. He is highlighting our crying need for inner, spiritual cleanliness. Flat on your face or sitting up, there is a stance to be taken here, mentally and spiritually that is to do with our old companion, sin. Contemporary thought tells us that we are all basically good and that we come under influences that make us do bad things. Do not be deceived. Sin is alive and well in the 21st Century. The same fallen conditions exist for us as for Adam, Noah, Abraham, St Francis and John Wesley. To say sin does not exist is to live in denial, *"If we claim to be without sin, we deceive ourselves and the truth is not in us."* 1 John 1:8

Oswald Chambers puts it beautifully; "Once we realize that it is through the salvation of Jesus Christ that we are made perfectly fit for the purpose of God, we will understand why Jesus Christ is so strict and relentless in His demands. He demands absolute righteousness from His servants, because He has put into them the very nature of God." In Acts 17, Paul issues a command from God, for "all men everywhere to repent." v 30. It is significant that whenever the word repent is found in the Bible, especially when used by Jesus, it is nearly always in the imperative. Repentance is a transforming act. As soon as people have heard the Gospel, they are commanded to repent, leaving only the choice of whether to obey or disobey. It is as critical as that.

There is a lot of hard stuff here to get our heads round. I would suggest a pause for prayer, to open up to the Lord, to supply to Him your willingness to repent of the things He'll bring to your notice. He will supply the power for you to do it, so that you can turn right away from these things and step out with Him in the direction He indicates for you, refreshed and renewed.

CHAPTER 9   " WHY ? .... FOR THE SAKE OF - "

Forgiveness

" .... so that I might forgive and raise you up to walk even more upright lives, pleasing and serving Me ?"   'Words' Five E

This next clause is wonderfully uplifting. There is no mention of punishment, which our sinfulness really deserves. Notice He does not say 'Why are so few of you willing to confess your sins?", although we cannot receive our forgiveness unless we are repentant. God yearns to forgive in order to *" raise you up to walk even more upright lives, pleasing and serving Me."* He knows that repentance might be hard for us, so He motivates, encourages and enables us to meet His requirements.

What then is all this confession and forgiveness for? So that we will experience the 'feel-good' factor? Not primarily, no, but so that God may lift us to higher levels of Christian living and service for Him, to improve what we are and what we do for Him. Making us righteous so that we can please Him, as He designed us to. His forgiveness is full, not limited or constrained and we all have need of it for the health of our souls and, incredibly, our bodies. Selwyn Hughes, in a recent book, 'Christ Empowered Living', has this to say on the subject of forgiveness, following repentance; "Human beings commit three types of offences. One is an offence against another person. Another is an offence against society. The third is an offence against God. The offence that needs forgiveness is the offence committed against God through maintaining an attitude of independence. Only God can forgive this kind of sin. This is one of the prerogatives of Deity. That was how people first began to realise that Jesus Christ was God on earth: He forgave sins. .... Look again at the cross. Christ died so that you might be forgiven." I couldn't put it any better. I can only echo Selwyn's plea; "So go to Him now and by faith take from Him the forgiveness of your sins." God longs to give it to you.

Fulfillment

".... and fulfilling the deepest desires of your own hearts?" 'Words' Five E

It is only by fulfilling the desires of God's heart that we fulfil our own! Because He made us, God knows precisely what the very deepest desires of our hearts are. They are for Him. Someone has flippantly talked about the 'God-shaped' hole inside each one of us which is empty until it is filled with love for Him. In the 3rd century AD St Augustine wrote; "You have created us for yourself, and our heart cannot be stilled until it finds rest in you. "

Adam and Eve lived at first in a perfect relationship with God. This is the blueprint for how it should be. Then sin intervened and it all went horribly wrong. They had replaced God at the centre of their lives with self, so they ran away from Him instead of towards Him. We are still doing that. In our unredeemed state, we cannot do anything else, because, as we know, holiness and sin cannot mix, they repel each other, like oil and water. Without God in His rightful place at the very core of our lives, we are off-centre, restless, lacking equilibrium and as with all living things, we are constantly seeking equilibrium. We can find temporary relief in all sorts of things, Christian or non-Christian, but they will only soothe for a while. God and only God can give us the fulfillment and stability our hearts crave and then only when we invite His attentions and address the sin in our lives. The choice is ours, which is why He pleads with us here to seek His forgiveness, rather than commanding us, as He has done elsewhere.

This is the God who loved us so much that He gave up His one and only Son to the most awful suffering and death to secure the way for sinners to be reconciled to Him. He stands by and asks us to seek His forgiveness because He longs to shower us with it. Then He asks so little in return, just that we would serve and please Him first all our lives, through which we are fulfilled.

CHAPTER 10
"HOW? .... TO THE GLORY OF GOD."

Introduction

1) "How little of My glory shines out from your churches. How much of your paltry glory masks My wonderful glory, when you pursue worldly ends instead of heavenly ones." 'Words' Four A

2) "How is it that I look for the fulfillment of My creation and I do not see it?" 'Words' Four E

3) "How can you walk in defeat when I have given you feet to skip lightly in blissful joy through this life and all its troubles?" 'Words' Five F

Again we have three distinct pieces to look at in this Chapter, their three key thoughts being glory, creation and triumph. Julian of Norwich saw in her Revelations of Divine Love, "three properties of God : life, love and light; " Uncreated Himself, He is the creator of everything good. Eternally triumphant, He has victory in all things.

In this chapter we will be looking at His Glory, contrasting it to our glory ; then at our churches, and our pursuits, asking if they are worldly or heavenly ; we shall ponder the phrase, 'the fulfillment of creation' and we shall consider the implications of the demand that we walk in victory, not defeat. After the heavy demands of the previous chapter, it will be good to lift our spirits, raise our eyes and soak in the wonder of the glory of our God.

If you go to the dictionary for a definition of the word glory, you will find that another word derived from it comes first - glorify. Let us glorify God, in our minds and hearts as well as in our lives and voices. Let us raise Him high on our praise and give Him the worship due to His name, for He is worthy. His glory supersedes anything we can describe or imagine. Glory be to God!

His Glory

"How little of My glory shines out from your churches."   'Words' Four A

Throughout scripture God gives us an intimation of the glory that is His, a hint of what we will find when we reach heaven and see Him fully. A Biblical definition of God's glory means the exhibition of His divine attributes or the radiance of his presence. To return to the vision recorded by Julian of Norwich, she says " I was able to touch, see and feel some of the three properties of God on which the strength and meaning of the whole revelation is based; .... The properties are these: life, love and light. .... These properties belonged to a single goodness; " These three properties of God, life, love and light underpin God's glory. I particularly like the idea that the properties also belong to 'a single goodness'. There is something very powerful about that little phrase. It goes beyond the mere statement that God is good. His is a unique goodness.

Glory is both physical and spiritual, as is seen in *Luke 2:9 "the glory of the Lord shone around them"* or in *John 17:22*, where it refers to the glory of the Father that Jesus gave to his disciples. As for the saints, glory culminates in their bodily transformation to the likeness of their glorified Lord, see Phil. 3:21. From Genesis Chapter 1, however, through to Revelations Chapter 22, the Bible glows with the reflected glory of God, in the accounts of His creation, His dealings with mankind, Jesus' coming and the birth and development of the worldwide Christian church. It draws our attention to the majesty and splendour of God's glory, to its riches, its manifestations and astounding beauty, to how it is revealed in earth and heaven and how it fills the heavenly sanctuary for which we are bound. This is just a little summary of what constitutes God's glory. I could never tell it all, it is so vast and wonderful. It remains to say, we should glorify God so that His glory can shine out more brightly to the world.

CHAPTER 10   " HOW ? .... TO THE GLORY OF GOD "

Our churches, our glory

"How little of My glory shines out from your churches. How much of your paltry glory masks My wonderful glory, ..."   *'Words' Four A*

This is not a question. God is making a statement here. It is His assessment of the current state of the church. Because we regard the church as 'ours' things are not as they should be. It is sad that God has to tell us that so little of our church activity brings glory to Him. We have reduced its beam to a weak, little glimmer when it should be a dazzling blaze. We need to show God's glory by our lives and by the action and the stand of the church.

How can a paltry glory mask a more powerful glory? Ponder an eclipse of the sun and there you have the answer. The moon, having no light of its own, borrows its light from the sun. Yet, in the course of its orbiting, it drifts between the earth and the sun, blotting out all but a fringe of rays, throwing the earth into deep shadow and making itself appear as a dark, featureless lump. We do have a glory, bestowed by God, but ours looks paltry in comparison with His. Yet, we persist in blocking God's glory with ours. Why?

What kind of church does God require? Look at the *'Words' Set One D* - *'I want My church to* **reverberate** *with My praise and My power.'* What a word! The idea is of a light or heat source or a sound being continuously echoed or bounced back to its receptors. The church should be constantly echoing God's praise, reflecting the light and power of God's glorious presence into all the dark corners of the world. To me a church that reverberated with God's power and praise would be an exciting place to be. There are plenty of ways to reverberate. It doesn't have to imply hyperactivity. What it does exclude though, is deadness or being lukewarm. In Revelations God tells the church in Laodicea; *"I know your deeds, that you are neither cold nor hot. I wish you were either one or the other! So, because you are lukewarm - neither hot nor cold - I am about to spit you out of my mouth."* Rev 3:15-16. God's intention here, I believe, is not to reject us, but to encourage us to move from the good things we are already doing into the very best that we could do.

Our pursuits

"How much of your paltry glory masks My wonderful glory, when you pursue worldly ends instead of heavenly ones."   'Words' Four A

There are, of course, many ways we can pursue worldly ends. We are being sharply cautioned here. Our aims have to be qualitatively different to those of the world. If our focus is on God and on the needs of His Kingdom, on the necessity to spread the gospel in order that the maximum number of people are saved in our generation, and the next generation are properly prepared for their share of the task, then we have no business nor any time to be involving ourselves in any worldly aims. We should only be pursuing heavenly ends.
Currently there is one particular aim that I feel is having the greatest detrimental effect on the church. This is the urge to be 'politically correct'. I want to make it clear, that there are aspects of this movement that are positive and beneficial. I have no argument with the strong measures being implemented to prevent such things as child abuse within organisations, including the church, or sensible regulations concerning health and safety. Political correctness, however, is a forceful ideology entirely consistent with our times. Outwardly it seems a very good thing, but it is nevertheless, the inevitable result of the strident demands for rights that dominate our society so much. When the church adopts such a flawed, worldly tool to resolve spiritual issues, then it is failing in its prime task of presenting the Gospel of truth and salvation to the world. Political correctness may save a few faces, but it will save no-one eternally and it is only through salvation and God's truth that real equality and justice can be attained. So the next time you or your minister or church council are tempted to opt for a politically correct resolution or decision, stop and ask yourselves why you are doing so. Are you pursuing worldly ends, or heavenly ones?

CHAPTER 10   " HOW ? .... TO THE GLORY OF GOD "

The fulfillment of the creation

"How is it that I look for the fulfillment of My creation and I do not see it?"
'Words' Four E

God set up His creation as the means of fulfilling His love. It is for this completion that He looks and is disappointed. It seems that we have messed it up so badly that it cannot achieve this end. God is a relational being and therefore, we, being made in His image, are also relational beings. The most important relationship to any human being, Christian or non-Christian, is their relationship to God, who made them. You can choose to deny it, but then you have to live with the consequences. Everything God has done and is doing is geared to one aim, to satisfy His love for us all. *Set Four* as a whole paints for us in broad brushstrokes a wide panorama of God's creativity. In the statement in Four E there is the huge sweep of the broadest brushstroke containing God's motivation for all His work. Our response completes this work, completes Him! If you doubt this, turn to Romans Chapter 8: 14-24. Eugene Peterson puts it beautifully ; *"The created world itself can hardly wait for what's coming next. Everything in creation is being more or less held back. God reins it in until both creation and all the creatures are ready and can be released at the same moment into the glorious times ahead." vv 19-21 'The Message.'*

God is poised and ready to go, but we are not. He is frustrated by our reluctance to open up to Him fully in love and by our selfishness which denies access to the sanctifying work of His Holy Spirit in our lives. As well as making us relational beings, He has made us volitional beings, with freedom of choice. What a risky thing to do! But a race of robots or string puppets coerced into obedience could never satisfy the God who is love. Only a full, free giving of our love in return for His can satisfy His love.

   " How long," He cries, *"how long will it be before you wake up My children, to your part in My plan and start to play your part fully? How long?"*

Feet to skip

"How can you walk in defeat when I have given you feet to skip lightly in blissful joy through this life and all its troubles?"   *'Words' Five F*

In a way this question sums up the rest of the *'Words'*. Defeat and triumph are the negative and positive sides of the issues raised. We have a choice in all the circumstances we meet in life, as to how we will react and behave. God is calling us here to choose the positive, triumphant way.

We need to entrench deep into our thinking the conviction that God's people are unbeatable. We may suffer setbacks and the church, as we know, is under tremendous pressure, but we can have confidence in what God promises and in His ability and willingness to equip us fully for the work ahead. This requires a deep level of commitment to God and His purposes here on earth, and a disregard of self or what we might term our own rights. We have to be prepared to go all the way in whatever it is God asks of us.

If like me you'd have no trouble skipping blissfully if you had no problems, this might be easier, but none of us can avoid trouble and when it arises, we tend to drag our feet, metaphorically speaking. The Christian however has a valuable weapon in their armoury - joy! Such joy is both a fruit of the Spirit, as in Galatians 5:22 and a gift of God. It is independent of circumstances and dependent on God. It is what St Paul experienced and it enabled him to say he had learned the secret of being content in any and every circumstance. The joy of the Lord resides deep within the soul, enabling us to cope victoriously and to have faith and patience when solutions are a long time coming or situations drag on and on painfully.

Given all that we know about God, how then can we walk in defeat? The world, in its mocking mode would like to make us believe we're a bunch of losers, but what the world refuses to acknowledge is its need of God and of salvation. Where Christians are standing firm and witnessing to the truth of God's salvation, sometimes despite awful consequences, people are flocking to the church. This is God's victorious activity in the world.

CHAPTER 11

"ABSENT FATHERS"

Introduction

No other god can satisfy all our needs.

"He had always been there .... A constant in a constantly shifting world."
Sammarah's Garden

We move now into a more contemplative mood. In this part of the book we will be taking a lot of the root material from the five inspirational stories that accompany the sets of *'Words'*. For these next five chapters, I also want to take the book's title and consider, meditatively, an issue that links it with the subject of each individual chapter. Here, we are considering the thought that **no other god can satisfy all our needs**.

One poignant image runs throughout all the stories, that of absent fathers. In the cases of Sam, Sammarah, the boy and Jason the fathers have absented themselves. Peter, the crusader, is banished at a tender age from his parental home, effectively leaving him fatherless and the fathers are so absent in the last story, *"The Six Trees"*, as to be not even mentioned, with the exception of the baby's father, who is referred to anyway as the 'husband'. What should we make of this? I think it is a sad reflection of our times. Fatherhood was a very important concept in Biblical times. In my opinion, it is woefully undermined nowadays. It would be all to our advantage to recapture its importance in our present troubled times.

This chapter guides us away from the negatives to focus on the positive aspects of God's fathering, to the God who alone is sufficient for all our needs, whatever damage is done to us by our upbringing or by those whom we ought to have been able to trust as children. It also contains an analysis of the consequences of becoming separated or alienated from God by our own choice and actions, in contrast to the situation that obtains when we take up our rightful position as God's children, heirs with Jesus of His heavenly kingdom. What it does not cover in any detail, as these areas are more than amply dealt with in many other books, are the effects of abuse, poor parenting or of growing up in dysfunctional families. In passing, it has been observed that Jesus' family was a typical 'dysfunctional' family! Born to a very young, single Mum, brought up with a 'step-dad' and lots of step brothers and sisters, homeless, a refugee at a very early age and maybe even obliged to work as a youngster to contribute to the family finances. Like so many youngsters, He went missing, nearly giving His parents heart failure till He was found alive and well! Then He embarked on a 'career' that they didn't anticipate, couldn't understand and felt thoroughly unhappy about. How many parents and Grandparents will be smiling a wry smile as they identify with all this?

Finally, we will also examine the concept of 'child of God', debunking the misconception that all human beings are automatically God's children, giving a clear definition of exactly who are children of God, how to attain that status and the demands it subsequently entails.

CHAPTER 11 ABSENT FATHERS

Satisfying our needs

".... he did resent it, especially when he saw other boys being given more ...."
2 K. B.

One of the names of our God is El-Shaddai. "The traditional interpretation of the Hebrew name El-Shaddai is this: 'God who is sufficient' or 'God the enough' What a beautiful word picture this presents of the infinite resources of an Almighty God." [Selwyn Hughes]. I had always thought another of God's names portrayed Him as sufficient - Jehovah Jireh, my provider, until I read Selwyn Hughes' excellent exegesis on the subject. Here's what he says about Jehovah Jireh; "God provides a multiplicity of things for the subjects of His creation. He provides the food we eat, the air we breathe, and the light by which we see. But what is His greatest provision? It is atonement for our sin. The term Jehovah Jireh carries with it clear intimations of Calvary. It is a signpost directing us to the cross. " Jehovah Jireh names God as our Saviour, giving Himself for us, that we might live eternally.

You may or may not be familiar with Maslow's hierarchy of human needs. It starts with what he classifies as physiological needs, those basic, mainly bodily needs for food and drink, air, light, warmth and so-on. It moves up through safety-security needs which are best defined as the need for a secure environment free from overwhelming threat where we can feel physically and emotionally safe. Further up the hierarchy come social needs, to be accepted, to have a sense of belonging and enjoy friendships. After this come our needs for esteem and status, making us feel good about ourselves, especially when we receive recognition, attention and appreciation. Only when our lower needs are satisfied, claims Maslow, can our highest need, for self-actualisation be met. This can be defined as our need to realise our inner potential, to become fully the person we know we could be. For the Christian this need is fulfilled when we become the person God made us to be. There are multitudinous reasons why people do not attain the final stage fully, or get stuck at different levels, to do with culture, upbringing, the society they live in and so-on. God intends us all to reach the top though. He is not like the Victorians, with their lower and higher orders and everyone knowing their place. He does not discriminate, saying, 'that person will reach level five whereas that person will only get to level two'! So why don't we all achieve that goal of self-actualisation? I believe it is to do with our expectations, of God, and of our fellow men.

What I am about to say can be extremely liberating. No human being can ever meet your needs entirely. Only God can do that. If you are looking for satisfaction, especially of your higher needs for self-esteem or self-actualisation, solely in your human relationships, then you are going to be disappointed to a lesser or greater degree. I am not saying that we cannot meet each others' needs at all. When God created Adam, He saw that it was not good for him to be alone, so He created Eve to be his helper and companion. However, in the initial set-up in the garden of Eden, that human relationship worked within their perfect relationship with God. He gave them each other as part of His fulfillment of their needs. Unfortunately, they chose to sin and consequently we all have to live in the imperfect, fallen world that resulted from their sin. This does not alter the fact that there is only one way that all our needs can be fully met and that is through God, not through each other. Once we get our heads round the idea that we should look to God to satisfy our needs, we find we can relax and relate to each other in a totally new way. We are no longer hooked on the unrealistic expectation that others should gratify all our demands for approval or appreciation. Our worth, our reward and our satisfaction is supplied by God. Then we can turn, in His strength, to helps others meet their needs.

Of course, some people attempt to satisfy their needs for security, self-worth and self-realisation through other means like a career, hobbies, amusements, sexual conquests or different pursuits. None of these will satisfy completely. Nor will a constant round of trying new things. All of these can be seen as 'other gods', or 'other lovers' as in *Set Two D* of the *'Words'*. No other god, no other lover will ever give you what God, the Captain and lover of your soul can, and longs, to give you, which is complete fulfillment of all that you are, all your good and righteous desires and the highest you could possibly aim for or achieve.

CHAPTER 11 ABSENT FATHERS

Marginalising God

"She broke his heart more often than she pleased him." Sammarah's Garden

This is something we do all too frequently in all kinds of situations, not just when we are attempting to gratify ourselves without God. From the outset let me stress that God is always present in our lives. He is always at our side or closer, no matter how we may be feeling and He never permits anything that will permanently damage His children's eternal souls. He will allow painful situations, because we grow through them, and learn important lessons, especially how to trust Him!

The effect of deliberately marginalising God is described through the character Idral in the opening paragraph of *" Sammarah's Garden"*. Who is Idral representative of? Surely it is God? This is what we do to God when we push Him out of His rightful place in the centre of our lives. We break His heart! Maybe not literally, but more in the figurative sense, as when we use the expression, to say someone is broken-hearted over a disappointment or a trauma. In this way, God is heartbroken over the capriciousness of His beloved children, when they are careless of His affection and indifferent to His love. And just look at the effect on Sammarah of her denial. All she can make of herself is a hardened exterior, with the real Sammarah locked up tight inside, frustrated and unfulfilled. This is what we do to ourselves when we absent God from our lives. We may continue to do a good job at work, keep a neat, tidy house, produce an attractive garden and raise well-adjusted and well-behaved children. We may even be very successful materially, and in our contribution at church. People may look up to us admiringly and hold us up as an example to their own recalcitrant offspring! None of which is intrinsically wrong, but if it is achieved entirely by our own effort and does not have God central to it then it is, as Paul said *"only a resounding gong or a clanging cymbal."* Note, he was talking about lacking in love. What is marginalising God, absenting Him from our lives, if it is not a lack of love? Our lives are desperately impoverished without the God who made us and loves us at the heart of them, but His is impoverished too. He clearly laments the lack of a full, satisfying relationship with us, His children, in *Set Two* of these *'Words'*. Put these alongside Jesus' affirmation to Nicodemus; *"God so loved the world that he gave his one and only Son, that whoever believes in him shall not perish but have eternal life. For God did not send his Son into the world to condemn the world, but to save the world through him." John 3:16-17* How could a God who loves in that way not be affected by our refusal or failure to respond to Him with love? Although in no way can we diminish Him, and nothing of His ultimate nature can be reduced or changed in any way, we can still impoverish His life and our own by the paucity of our response to His great love.

In *"The Crusader"* Peter found that; *"What sustained him through those last years of his life was the look that passed between him and his father that day on the battlefield. From that look he knew that his father had suffered the pain of separation as much as he had."* Just take a moment to absorb what this is telling us. God suffers the pain of separation from us caused by our unrepented sin, our refusal to respond to Him in love, just as much as we feel the pain of it, if we're honest with ourselves.

CHAPTER 11 ABSENT FATHERS

The Father-Heart of God

".... the young man glances at his father .... Their eyes meet and hold. It seems for a second that the noise of battle recedes and time stands still. Deep within that look is recognition that they both love each other very much. Then the father gives the minimalist of nods, the son slips away safe and free and the father is engulfed and slaughtered by the enemy."   The Crusader

Floyd McLung uses this phrase as the title for an excellent book. It is so entirely fitting for what I want to say that I have borrowed it as the heading of this section. We hold a very special place in the Father's heart, - 'beloved'. In the extract from *"The Crusader"* Peter has been recalled from his undemanding way of life as a scribe in a Monastery and made to fight in battle alongside his father. As the story tells us, at this stage; *"There is little love lost between him and his father."* Peter obeys his father's command out of a sense of obligation and duty. Some of this father's behaviour helps us to clarify our understanding of God's loving operations in our lives. Although he is obliged to punish Peter for a youthful misdemeanour, there is still a strong residue of love buried deep in his heart. In that last eyeballing second, there was forgiveness, reconciliation and impartation, but over all these there was the triumph of love. It is this triumph of love that gives us a window directly into the Father-heart of God. This is where Peter's father teaches us about the strength and depth of the love God has in His heart for us. It is love so strong that it endures despite the worst that we can possibly do.

Now all Peter had done was scrump a few apples, hardly the crime of the century you might say. However, if we use the misdemeanour as a representation of sin we begin to see where we are going. All sin is equally bad, putting an impassable gulf between us and God. The estrangement between Peter and his father epitomizes this gulf. But, because God has a Father's heart, He cannot live with such a situation. In spite of all that we do in violation of His law, we are still His beloved creation and just as any parent yearns over their naughty children, so God yearns over us, only His yearning is magnified beyond all we could imagine. He can do nothing however, if we are not willing to renounce our sin. Peter could have refused to obey his father's summons, but he didn't. Albeit resentfully, he responded and found that his sense of obligation and duty came to his aid so that he could not only do as his father asked, but eventually be reconciled with him.

Extracting the spiritual lesson from this, we may not want to obey the Father's summons to war, to fight the battle in our own lives against sin, the world and the devil, but, if only out of duty and obligation we make the first move, we find that we are taken straight to the core of the problem. Simultaneously, we find that we are not alone. The Father is there with us, as close as the very air we breathe.

God will chastise us when we do wrong, because He has a Father's heart for us. He loves us enough, as good earthly fathers love their children , not to let us get away with behaviour that is wrong and therefore will harm us, maybe not physically, but certainly morally and spiritually. The writer to the Hebrews exhorts his readers not to forget *"that word of encouragement that addresses you as sons: "My son, do not make light of the Lord's discipline, and do not lose heart when he rebukes you, because the Lord disciplines those he loves, and he punishes everyone he accepts as a son." Hebrews 12:5-6*

Strange thinking in the eyes of the world. We're telling them God loves them in one breath, while in the next breath telling them He punishes all those He loves. However, if we read on, thereby putting it into context, we find this: - *"Endure hardship as discipline; God is treating you as sons. For what son is not disciplined by his father?"* This matter of discipline is just as much a part of the Father-heart of God as the immense love we have seen that He carries for us. In fact, it arises out of that love, make no mistake about it.

So to sum up, the idea of the Father-heart of God encompasses two main facets. One is that God loves us as a father loves his child, tenderly, compassionately, enduringly but set beside this is the other facet, that this love is tough enough to chastise us when we need it, in order that we come to the perfection He created us to attain. We are ready now to move on to the next section, where we will examine in greater depth what it means to be a child of God, who loves us with a Father's heart.

Chapter 11 Absent Fathers

Children of God

"A little girl, one of his brother's children, skips past him, stops, turns and regards him seriously.
Are you my Uncle Peter?" she quizzes him.
"I am indeed"
"Tell me a story then," she demands, proprietorially settling herself on his lap.
He thinks a bit and then tells her about a funny incident he had with a pig that wouldn't be driven to market and ran amok all through the cottage of the old lady who owned it. The little girl enjoyed the story and demanded more. He obliged with several more, until a nursemaid came looking for the child for a meal and bustled her away with much telling off, for disappearing, for wasting the gentleman's time, for getting her clothes dirty and her hair messed and so-on."
The Crusader

Children feature largely throughout the stories and I chose the heading 'Children of God' because I specifically want to explore the idea of being a **child** of God. There are two elements to this section, one is about becoming a child of God and the other is to do with our role as children of God. Contrary to popular belief, not every person, regardless of religious standing is a child of God. We have to become children of God through adoption. *"In love he predestined us to be adopted as his sons through Jesus Christ, in accordance with his pleasure and will"*. Ephesians 1:4-5 We just come as we are, give ourselves to Jesus as we are, confessing our sin and our need for forgiveness and He takes us to the Father to be made His children. It is instant acceptance and there is nothing to pay. All we have to give is our life; *"whoever loses his life for my sake will find it"* Matthew 10:39 We can only have life if we are prepared to give up our lives. It's a strange dichotomy I know, but I also know it's the only way it works. To borrow a picture from a Social Work text book that I picked up on a second hand book stall; "Adoption is a legal process, but it is also a very human affair. The adoption order obtained in court marks only the end of the beginning. Happy adoptions develop and grow like every other relationship. That is why a book about adopting a child should not stop dead outside the door of the court but ought to accompany the new family along the road for a while as it sets out on its great adventure." [Kornitzer] Although the book deals with adoption in a worldly sense, not in a spiritual sense, there is a legality about our adoption as children of God. It is a spiritual law that we cannot become His any other way.

Better still though, is her view of the adoption as the end of the beginning. Having *become* a child of God, we then have to learn to live *as* a child of God. Some churches are very good at helping us along the way, some are not. Selwyn Hughes puts it like this; "we evangelicals are good obstetricians but bad pediatricians. We are good at bringing people into the Christian faith but we are not good at nurturing them." Perhaps your church is different to this. Or maybe it has a strong teaching ministry, but only to the same faithful few year in and year out.

Look again at the little girl. She scampers along, without any clear idea of where she is going, does a double take when she sees Peter and plonks herself trustfully on his lap. God is asking for the same kind of trust from us, uncomplicated and childlike. Having settled herself down, she does not switch off. The story described is not a simple docudrama about raising pigs, which would very quickly bore her. It is a tale full of movement, humour and nuances of meaning, all of which she is capturing in her mind, sifting, considering and learning from. This is called active listening. Notice she promptly demanded more. Although she had to work to gain her enjoyment, it had its own satisfaction. So it is with becoming a child of God, we have to work at it.

One vitally important point needs making here before we go any further. The repentance we undergo at our initial conversion is not all the repentance we ever need to carry out. Regular and frequent confession of and repentance from the ongoing sin that so besets our lives, even after we have become Christians, is essential for healthy growth and discipleship. God does not save us, then leave us to get on with it. He saves us in order to make us what He intended us to be. This is the great adventure.

CHAPTER 11 ABSENT FATHERS

Abiding in Him

"For Netta it was a bigger step of faith, but she felt she could take it and she was to find that Mrs Brown would not disappoint her."   2 K. B.

Apart from the fact that there are hundreds of books advising and teaching us about every aspect of the Christian life, there is one very good way I believe that we can learn how to live as a child of God. We have a precedent, Jesus Himself. Read through John's Gospel and see how Jesus related to His Father. It gives us a composite picture of all that is necessary. Jesus describes their relationship as 'oneness'. In everything He consulted with and submitted to the Father. They know each other, they honour each other, they glorify one another, love each other, and work together. Jesus does God's will, obeys His commands and completes His work. He has been taught by God and He shows us what the Father is like. God authorizes the Son, setting Him apart, granting His requests, approving of Him and remaining with Him always. He also honours Jesus' followers.

One word sums up Jesus relationship with God, 'abiding'. Jesus said quite a lot about abiding, because it was what He did best. Not so many of the books teach us how to sit at God's feet in humble adoration and deep, comforting companionship. It is what the little girl is doing as she nestles on Peter's knee, soaking up his stories. In *"2 K. B."*, Netta shows all the signs that she is going to 'abide' in Mrs Brown's classroom, but what of Sam? Already his discontent and restlessness are evident. He wants to by-pass the system to get what he wants. Letting people think they can by-pass the need to abide in God yet still reap His rewards is irresponsible and unscriptural.

The Biblical teaching on the subject of abiding is found almost exclusively in John's Gospel. In John 6:56 Jesus foretells the Eucharist, *"He who eats My flesh and drinks My blood abides in Me and I in him."* The next two references are addressed to *"the Jews who had believed him."* He tells them *"If you abide in My word, you are My disciples indeed. And you shall know the truth, and the truth shall make you free." John 8:31* NKJ. They don't like that. They're not slaves, according to them, but Jesus shows them otherwise,

"Most assuredly, I say to you, whoever commits sin is a slave of sin. And a slave does not abide in the house for ever, but a son abides forever." 8:34-35 NKJ

In John 14:16, He brings the Holy Spirit into the picture; *"And I will pray the Father, and He will give you another Helper, that He may abide with you for ever."* NKJ. God gives the Spirit in order that He may abide within us, right where He wants to be, for ever. The last six comments on abiding all come from Chapter 15, verses 4, 6, 7, 9 and 10. Whether Jesus actually delivered them all in one go or whether it is an amalgam by John of lots of His teaching I do not know. Taken together however, they are pretty powerful.

We are being instructed not to look to Jesus just for our salvation and for access to the Father, but we are also to love Jesus, as much as we love the Father. This is a timely reminder. It might be easy for us to get so hooked up on the desire to abide in and with God, the Father, that we forget His beloved Son, who, after all, has made such a colossal sacrifice for us. Jesus of course is **the** Son of God, as we know, but what does scripture tell us about Him vis a vis sonship ? *"For those God foreknew he also predestined to be conformed to the likeness of his Son, that **he might be the firstborn among many brothers."** Rom. 8:29* Imagine that! Jesus, Son of God, becomes our brother once we are adopted as God's children , *"our fellowship is with the Father and with his Son, Jesus Christ." 1 John 1:3* I know sisters and brothers argue and squabble, but there is a tie of love too deep to be destroyed between most siblings. The tie of love we have to Jesus, our heavenly 'brother' is stronger still because He is also the Lord who saved us!

So being a child of God means abiding in God Our Father and in His Son, Jesus Christ, and, through the action of the Holy Spirit in our souls, allowing them to abide within us. As Oswald Chambers wrote, the cross " is not a gate we pass right through; it is one where we abide in the life that is found there." Jesus said *'abide in Me'*. He is, therefore, the place where we are at one with God, just as He was at one with God.

CHAPTER 12

" ABUNDANCE "

Introduction

No other god provides for us as our God does.

"It looked as though this new school was going to be good. The other two girls said Mrs Brown was a lovely teacher, one had an older sister who'd been in Mrs Brown's class two years ago and had loved it."   2 K. B.

We are still considering El Shaddai, God the Enough, but we are moving here more into the material realm. Mrs Brown gives us a useful thumbnail sketch of God the Enough. The environment she creates in her classroom is exemplary, not simply in the material provisions but also in the ethos and atmosphere. God created an ideal world at first but it is spoiled now and any ideal worlds we try to produce will always be marred by our imperfection. This does not detract from the fact that God makes abundant provision for all our needs in this life. His abundance knows no limit. Cast your mind back to the 'Words', Set Two and remember what He said there :-

"I desire a romantic relationship with each one of you, My children. I long to be as intimate with you as the very air you breathe. I rejoice over you with singing, My delight is in you and you are desirable to Me. I long to adorn you with the adornments of My love, with gifts and garments, graces and a new name known only to Me. I am an aggresive lover, pursuing you, My beloved children across the plains of Earth and Heaven, seeking to save, redeem, protect and nurture you. I am deeply hurt when you are indifferent to My love and careless of My affection. I long for you to reject all your other lovers and to remember your first love for Me, so that I can gather you close into My arms and whisper My endearments to you. Above all else I desire

you with all My heart and long for you to desire Me with all your heart."

I find it helpful to read a set of these *'Words'* as I have given them here, as a whole text, as well as in their component parts. They gain, if possible, even greater power and depth. This set nearly overwhelms you with the wealth of God's generosity. Here is a cornucopia of spiritual blessings, coupled with an extra-ordinarily passionate love.

God's love for us is a grand passion on a scale unseen anywhere else. It is a relationship in a quite different dimension to our human relationships, although He uses the same language to explain and describe it to us, because that is the only way we can understand it. Through it He lovingly pours out the full wealth of His blessings on us as His children, while at the same time, turning us into the fully mature, grown up Christians He intends us to be, able to respond from the depths of our hearts to our celestial lover.

You will be familiar with the saying 'What do you want first, the bad news or the good news?' We are going to start our section by section examination of this theme with the bad news, to get it out of the way, so that we can build up to the good news in the following sections and finish the chapter on a high note. The stories abound in images of abundance, but we cannot ignore the fact that not all of them are of good things. There is a thread that traces an abundance of bad things and clearly reflects a major aspect of our earthly existence. Without becoming depressed or wallowing in hopelessness, we do need to face up to this situation and learn to deal with it positively, in God's strength. This is all part of the victorious living He encourages us to adopt.

CHAPTER 12 ABUNDANCE

Abundance of bad

"This tree .... [rose] over the mess that had reigned so long at its roots and that had threatened to defeat the volunteers when they came to attack this last bit of desolation, their numbers depleted by the falling off of the less stalwart, fair weather friends of the project, and their spirits depressed at the tough challenge this last bastion had thrown them."   The Six Trees

The bad seems to stack up in abundance. I distilled five distinct aspects from the stories. They are, destructiveness; illegality or unethical actions; worthlessness; severe trials and woes; and threats. Taking the last story, *"The Six Trees"* words typifying destructiveness are bulldozed, sold off, demolished, dissipation, wrenched up, felled, and dead. Images of destruction from the other four stories include Sam breaking the pencils, the boy's rampage through Sammarah's garden, the deaths of Peter's parents and the burning of the small church in *"Two Churches"*.

Illegality can be seen in Sammarah diverting water from her neighbours, the boy using an illegal means of entry into the garden, the reference to illicit play in *"The Six Trees"*, and the old man's rent being 'years in arrears ' all of which are unjust, unethical or illegal in one way or another. So too is the harsh treatment meted out to Peter, although scrumping apples is strictly stealing. Then we have fire-setting in *"Two Churches"*, breaking and entering, and vandalism, all images connected with law-breaking and illegality.

Next is worthlessness, which I have alternatively labeled de-valuation. There are a lot of key words for this one, again from *"The Six Trees"*. They are awkward plot, not worth spending on, a bit of scrubland, scrubby field, unsightly hotchpotch, numbers depleted and, deserted by fair weather friends. No-one taking any notice of Netta's previous teacher is a telling picture of lack of respect, undervaluing a person. Sam's behaviour paints a portrait of a boy with no sense of the worth of others. The same is seen in Sammarah belittling her friend and Idral, but reciprocally in her friends deserting her when the boy attacks. On Peter's return, he finds no room for him at his old home. His brothers had stood in neutral detachment as he was punished, more concerned for their own skins. His father had dismissed him with cold, chilling words instead of being the person who should warmly champion him. Look finally at the meanness of the small church building, the mean-spiritedness of the Pastor's wife and the stereotypical attitude of the members of the big church in de-valuing the small church. Not a pretty picture is it so far?

By trials and woes, I mean severe disasters, tragedies and stubborn, resistant problems, ongoing painful, negative situations that many people have to learn to live with. Sam's overall situation, no Dad, Mum locking him out of the house, families like the boy's, in dire straits through poverty and injustice. The awfulness of war, the enduring frustration Chris feels about Jason, the regular nagging worry over money in the minds of the members of the little church and the spiritual starvation of the town.

In similar vein are the images of threat. A nearby town encroached, lumberjacks appeared wielding chainsaws, the mess threatened to defeat the volunteers. Sam would appear fairly threatening to another 6 year old as he glowers, grins unpleasantly, swaggers and pokes out his tongue. The boy, seething with anger, turns a knife on Sammarah. The enemy out-number Peter and his father on the battlefield and in *"Two Churches"* there is the threat of burn-out, not from the real fire, but from the hyper-activity of the one and the hyper-anxiety of the other.

All in all this could be a depressing catalogue if it weren't for the power of God to overcome such things. At one level, I believe it imparts realism to counteract the tendency in certain Christian circles to declare that the moment a person becomes a Christian all their troubles are over. Not only is this untrue, but at the least it is not helpful and at the worst, it can give rise to overwhelming feelings of guilt, failure and inadequacy. Another purpose is to show by contrast how much more powerful good is than bad, no matter how dreadful, and to show that bad can never, under any circumstances destroy the faithful who turn to God for their sustenance and relief in bad times, although they may be severely tested.

CHAPTER 12 ABUNDANCE

Greed

"In time she became seriously wealthy and acquired her valley property. It was then that she fell out with Idral. He wanted her to share her 'paradise garden' freely with all and sundry. She would not. To her surprise, for the first time ever, her closest friend turned against her"   Sammarah's Garden

Having established this, we turn now to the negative, destructive side of money and material wealth. Again, quite a lot is said on this theme throughout the stories. It is interesting that of all the bad things covered, this is singled out for special treatment in the *'Words' Set Five*, where materialism comes in for some specific disapprobation from the Lord.

Sometimes life can be expensive in more ways than just monetarily. Look at the 'cost' to Sam's Mum of changing his school. In her intransigence over her garden, Sammarah pays the price of losing her best friend. Peter's father lost not just a son, but also his beloved wife through his harsh sternness. On the surface of it, these don't seem to have much in common with Jesus' remarks, from Luke 12. He is warning us against material greed. Isn't there an element of material greed in the incidents above though? Whose interests is Peter's father looking after? He is Lord of the Manor, with a position to keep up. If he doesn't do so, he puts himself in danger of losing it all. It seems as though these considerations come before the welfare of his own son.

Jesus warns His listeners, *"Be on your guard against all kinds of greed;" Luke 12:15.* He's telling us that greed can take many guises, as I think we know. It is still frighteningly easy to fall into the greed trap, of putting our security and well-being into the accumulation of wealth and material possessions. So, rightly, Jesus teaches us that our lives do not *"consist in the abundance of our possessions", Luke 12:15* nor does our worth or status. We really do need to get that issue right. The abundance of our possessions is, I believe, from what God says in *Set Five* of the *'Words'*, given for an ulterior purpose, to help us, as a church and as individuals, to do all we can to spread the gospel.

Dearth of good

"Slumping back into the chair he mumbled sulkily "I'll have a sticker. My Mum won't be interested and she's not picking me up anyway." "   2 K. B.

I hesitated to use the word dearth as it is unfamiliar nowadays, but unlike lack, or scarcity, which mean the same thing, it encapsulates exactly what I want to say. Dearth of good is a phrase in the same vein as 'damning with faint praise'. There is good to commend, but there is so little of it. Key words associated with this section are neglect, difficulties or problems, misappropriation, exhaustion, and breakdown.

Starting with neglect, we have two instances in *"2 K. B."* Sam's Mum's neglect of him and the teacher at Netta's old school neglecting to maintain her classroom and her care of her pupils. Sammarah, in her youth, was neglectful of Idral, taking his care for granted and exploiting his generosity. There is woeful neglect of spiritual matters in both the churches in *'Two Churches'*, in favour of material, worldly things. From *'The Six Trees'* we get an overwhelming picture of neglect of the area that constitutes the park before its renovation. I think we can learn two lessons from this. One is that we can neglect our spiritual life in many ways, by not doing things like praying and meditating, repenting, giving and so-on, or by doing too many non-spiritual things that gobble up our time for the spiritual essentials. The second lesson, though, is that the situation is not lost, there is a remedy, symbolised by the regeneration of the park. We do not destroy our chances of restoration when we neglect our communion with God. It is recoverable, through repentance, which sometimes takes effort.

Misappropriation is most obvious in Sammarah's use of the valley water supply for her own private garden. It is also evident in the way both churches misdirect too much of their resources for a predominantly non-spiritual project in far away Sierra Leone, neglecting the spiritual needs of those right on their doorstep. With Sam, and with Peter, there is a sense of waste of potential or ability. How often do we misappropriate, or even squander,

Chapter 12 Abundance

precious resources given to us by God, monetary and other, for our own benefit or in schemes and projects that He has not sanctioned ?

Look at the sequence of events that led to the formation of the conservation society in *"The Six Trees"*. One hot summer night some youngsters set light to a bush, presumably sampling the illicit 'delights' of a cigarette. This prompted all the worthy citizens to call for 'something to be done', as they do. Note, they didn't offer to do anything themselves! The Curate set up his prayer group, well done that man, and immediately there was a response from the congregation. The society was formed and eventually adopted the park project. This is an allegory within an allegory. In it God is teaching us about the task of the church, where its focus should lie and where it has got its emphasis wrong. Everything we have in this life, including our abilities, constitute our worldly wealth. Unsurrendered we use it inappropriately, or we misappropriate it for wrong, selfish purposes. Surrendered, we are led by God to use our wealth gloriously for His purposes. Bear in mind here Jesus' timely warning *".... if you have not been trustworthy in handling worldly wealth, who will trust you with true riches?"* Luke 16:11.

We have three more aspects to consider. Difficulties or problems we can deal with quickly. They are not the trials and woes of the last section, nor are they dire or life threatening. They include such things as Netta's apprehension before starting her new school, the dilemma Peter finds himself in concerning his future, the limitations suffered by the small church and the minor hitches and set backs experienced by the volunteers in *'The Six Trees'*. They are another opportunity for us to prove to ourselves how much God supports and cares for us in all situations.

Exhaustion and breakdown can be examined together. They include Netta's old classroom, "tatty and neglected, everything shambolic and untidy", the boy's mother collapsing with exhaustion, Peter's family worn-out by a veil of tears, the Pastor of the small church sinking into despair, while his wife angrily drags him away. All these are incidences of people coming to the end of themselves, or of the inability of the world to provide for us, leading to breakdown or failure of relationships, of social order, of families and even of churches.

Abundance of good

"What a church this was! Stamping feet, loud Hosannas, groaning in prayer, weeping and singing .... No-one was turned away who came genuinely seeking the Lord and the membership grew and grew at an astounding rate. .... this church is strong and effective, not only in its own town, but in sending missionaries to other towns in the land. It is rich in spirit and in material wealth, both of which it spends liberally in spreading the Gospel of Jesus Christ. It has a fine new building, paid for by donations from its members as well as the original bequest, which is open and in use for the glory of God 24 hours a day, seven days a week, 52 weeks of the year."   Two Churches

At last we can revel in an abundance of good things. Note the change of tense in the passage above. It starts in the past tense, "What a church this was!", but quickly changes to the present tense, ".... this church is strong and effective ". Although it has a past, there is nothing passe or dead about this church. It is alive, vibrant and reverberating, just as God declares He wants His church to be.

What are the good things shown in the stories? Again they fall into five categories. These are affluence, beauty, pleasure, access and provision. *"I have come that they may have life and have it to the full"* Jesus assures us in John 10:10. It is a trite saying, 'count your blessings', but Selwyn Hughes cites a person who makes a habit of identifying five new blessings every morning when he first wakes up. I tried it one morning and found that I was spoiled for choice, even though I was in the middle of a painful, family trauma, which isn't fully sorted out yet! Yes, I can say, without a second's hesitation, Jesus has most definitely given me abundant life. As with all His promises, you can absolutely rely on this one. Come to Him and He will give you abundant life.

Taking affluence first, Sammarah's paradise garden itself is a product of affluence. Mrs Brown's classroom contains copious resources. Peter comes from a wealthy family; the big church is well off and is rich in activity. The park is an outcome of affluence. A picture builds up of immense amplitude in the natural world and in what man has made of it, setting aside pollution and depletion. There resources on this earth that exceed the needs of every generation, for as many generations as God intends to raise up, as long as no one generation is so greedy as to extract more than their fair share.

Beauty is our next image of abundance of good. Isaiah talks about the Messiah, *"He had no beauty or majesty to attract us to him, nothing in his appearance that we should desire him. He was despised and rejected by men, a man of sorrows, and familiar with suffering." Isaiah 53:2-3* Yet those of us who know Jesus would testify to His true inner beauty and radiance, which come from His Lordship and from His perfect relationship with the Father. He radiated God's glory and was entirely different and more beautiful than anyone we could ever know.

We come on now to pleasure. My real pleasure lies in doing what my Lord requires of me. I may take other pleasures, and they may amuse me temporarily, but they quickly pall. Look at our little friend Jason. What a pleasure he becomes. What delight his Mum, and Chris must feel because he has located the Jason he was made to be by God and started to fulfil that Jason properly, instead of in substitutionary activities that gratify his demand for excitement in unhealthy ways.

Access is an interesting concept. Very modern. Very politically correct, but also very much of God. He actually invented the idea. *"Then God said, "Let there be ...." " Gen. 1:3* Before He said that the earth had no form, therefore there was no access to it. Then He opened up the heavens and the earth and filled them with His teeming creation, leaving His crowning glory, mankind, till last, when all was in place for Him to give them access to it.

Access, with affluence, is part of provision, which is the last of our images of abundance of good. In *"2 K. B."* Mrs Brown provides a stimulating environment. Idral's calming presence brings peace and protection for the boy, for Sammarah and for the guests. A safe refuge is supplied for the child, Peter, when he is sent away. The new church and the new park are wonderful portraits of abundant provision for all who are seeking succour and refreshment. Taking the spiritual lesson from them, they illustrate the abundance that God can and does provide, for His beloved children.

Gifts and graces

"As a child she had delighted to snuggle up close to him and hear his stories. As a teenager she had anticipated his visits for the quirky presents he brought her that always fitted the particular phase or fad she was currently preoccupied with. As a young adult, coming out into the world bolstered up by false confidence, his quiet support was always there to be counted on."

Sammarah's Garden

This last section deals with some special components of God's abundant blessing and provision for us, referring to the *'Words'* rather than the stories, but entirely in keeping with this theme. The gifts mentioned in *Set Two* of the *'Words'* remind us of the spiritual gifts listed by Paul in several places. References to garments occur throughout the Scriptures, as in the letter to the church at Sardis, whose members had not *"soiled their clothes. They will walk with me, dressed in white, for they are worthy. He who overcomes will, like them, be dressed in white." Rev. 3:4-5*, or like the 24 elders later in Revelations, 4:4, who were also dressed in white. Paul talks of *" longing to be clothed with our heavenly dwelling, because when we are clothed, we will not be found naked. For while we are in this tent, we groan and are burdened, because we do not wish to be unclothed but to be clothed with our heavenly dwelling, so that what is mortal may be swallowed up by life." 2 Cor 5:2*. God is promising such garments, pleading with us to accept them, because He knows that we long for them in our hearts, long for the safety they give us and the assurance of His love and protection they bestow.

Then there are graces. What are these? Grace can be defined variously as meaning: charm, sweetness, loveliness, the attitude of God toward men, the method of salvation, the opposite of legalism, the impartation of spiritual power or gifts, or the freedom which God gives to men. It is also the means by which God has effected the salvation of all believers and is the sustaining force by which we persevere in our Christian walk. A gift of special grace is given to the humble.

Chapter 12 Abundance

And then, *'a new name known only to Me'* which Isaiah refers to and which is mentioned in Revelations; *"The nations will see your righteousness, and all kings your glory; you will be called by a new name that the mouth of the LORD will bestow."* Isaiah 62:2

" To him who overcomes, I will give some of the hidden manna. I will also give him a white stone with a new name written on it, known only to him who receives it." Rev 2:17 *"And I will also write on him my new name."* Rev 3:12

As we have already observed, in the Bible names had a far greater significance than they do today, signifying amongst other things, social position, specialised roles, particular relationships or specific events around the time of a person's birth. In Bible times if one person gave his own name to another, as when God gave his name to Israel, it signified the closeness of the union. The person and his name are practically equivalent, so that to take away a person's name was to destroy the person. In complete opposition to the removal of the name, and thereby, the person, God is promising here a new name, indicating a new significance and status for us, in Him. Add to all this, as if it wasn't enough anyway, His wishes expressed in *Set One*, to shower us with blessings, to bless us, to be with us always and everywhere and to pour out His Spirit on us. Put with them the gifts of His word, the Scriptures and His Word, Jesus, mentioned in *Set Three B* and His good and perfect law, *Set Three D* and you have still more evidence of the abundant goodness of our Lord towards us. We can really never be grateful enough for such great favour, but when we are grateful, He is even more delighted.

To conclude this Chapter then, we can say that no other god can satisfy us as our God can, no other god can meet our needs as He does, and no other god provides what our God provides for us. How can we chase after other gods when we have such a great, powerful, provider God as our God?

CHAPTER 13
"CONTROL"

Introduction

No other god is in control.

".... he alone had the power ...."   *Sammarah's Garden*

No other god is in control, of this world, of the next world, of the present or of the future. It may look as though other gods are in control, we may be led to think other gods, or other influences are in control, but it simply is not so. Only our God has full control over everything that happens, throughout His universe and throughout eternity. Nothing happens that He does not allow. Furthermore, He only allows events that will secure the ultimate good of the children He loves and who love Him, painful though those events may sometimes be. Creation is still marching to the beat of His drum, no matter what mankind does to destroy the earth or itself. I don't know about you, but in all the gloom, disaster, war and destruction we are faced with daily, I find this a tremendously uplifting and encouraging thought. What a great God we have. There can be no meeting ground for evil and the will of God, other than the battlefield, but His power and authority reign supreme and undefeated.

This chapter is about God's Kingdom, His rule of Law on earth, as in Heaven. As the main Bible reference I have taken Matthew 16:24-28:- "Then Jesus said to his disciples, *"If anyone **desires** to come after Me, let him deny himself, and take up his cross, and follow Me. For whoever **desires** to save his life will lose it, but whoever loses his life for My sake will find it. For what profit is it to a man if he gains the whole world, and loses his own soul? Or what will a man give in exchange for his soul? "* NKJ As so often I find, the New King James version brings out the depth and implications of a passage most powerfully. Look and meditate on the use of the word 'desires' here which I have put in bold. We should desire to follow Jesus, desire to be more like Him, desire to be entirely His! What is the alternative? To desire self-preservation. That way, says Jesus, leads to certain death. As Eugene Peterson puts it in *The Message* :- *"Then Jesus went to work on his disciples. "Anyone who intends to come with me has to let me lead. You're not in the driver's seat; **I am**."* Who is in control? You or God? Who is in control in the church? Us or God? Who should be in control?

Chapter 13 Control

Mrs Brown

"Sam considered his response. Her hand rested on the back of his chair. Somehow he knew he was on a losing wicket if he tried to get up and return to the other table. She meant him to stay by her and she wasn't going to have any arguments about it. He shrugged and pulled the colouring pencils nearer to him."

2 K. B.

To help us in our meditations on the subject of control I want to start by looking at Mrs Brown's initial encounter with Sam. It has much to teach us about God's dealings with us, especially when we are rebellious, an area we will look at more closely in Chapter 15. In the story we start by seeing it from Sam's point of view. "The woman who was their teacher" - ouch!, what a dismissive phrase. Sam is distancing himself from Mrs Brown's control while at the same time testing its strength. In Sam's assessment of the situation, she "was advancing on him", portraying hostility, which is counterbalanced by the "soppy smile" . To him, she's an iron fist in a kid glove. Many see God in this way, and react to God similarly to Sam; "he glowered " at her, waiting for the smile to fade. "She met his eyes and held them for a second or two. " Some challenge! Mrs Brown sees the real Sam behind the angry mask, just as God sees the real us behind any facade we might like to erect.

"You're Sam .... I'm Mrs Brown." There is far more here than simply establishing identities. She is letting Sam know his place in her scheme of things. He is not just one of the set of children that make up her class, or even that pesky nuisance from the school down the road! She affirms his status and personhood, as God does for all who are His, and longs to do for all who are not. Then she confirms her own identity, so that there will be no doubt about her role and status. From then on she's referred to as Mrs Brown, not "the woman". This done, "she passed on". She's seen and done all she needs to do for now and wastes no more time on unnecessary or ineffective business. Compare this with the teachers at Netta and Sam's previous schools, shouting orders over the babble, screaming and harrying. Isn't this how the world attempts to gain control? The urgent tyranny of 'duty', the strident demands of expediency and so-on. How dignified Mrs Brown seems by contrast. There's a lesson for us here, to move on, not to dally. If the work is finished, pass on to the next thing in God. If the task is not what you know God would have you do, pass on, give it no more than a prayer. God's got more suitable things for you to do and more appropriate people to do that task. This way, you are in control of your life, under God's direction, rather than external pressures controlling you.

Mrs Brown is a teacher who knows where she is going, what her aims and intentions are and how she is going to attain them. I am reminded of *Set One* of the *'Words'*, where God outlines what He wants, and the means by which He intends to achieve it. As with *Set Two*, in the last chapter, here is the whole of *Set One* for you :-

> *"I want to be the most important person in your lives. I want mankind everywhere to lift up holy hands and worship Me. I want all men to know My love, My care, My salvation. I want to shower you with My blessings. I want My people to turn from their selfish, sinful ways, to turn back to Me. I want to bless you, My people and be with you always, everywhere. I want to pour out My Spirit on you so that you can be My messengers, stewards and ambassadors in the world. I want My church to reverberate with My praise and My power so that the world sits up and takes notice."*

All through this set there is an underlying but. 'I want' says God, 'to do this, this and this, but, I can't." Why can't He do the things He wants to do? Because we will not surrender control to Him and submit fully to His control. This is an area I battle with daily. I prefer to maintain my independence, to reserve control of my life for myself. I'm sure all the saints down the ages would concur with that, but it is a battle we must engage in. When we assume control, things go wrong and there are negative, unhealthy consequences. When we surrender control to God, then only the right things can happen, and the consequences are positive and healthy, even if some events are traumatic and unpleasant at the time.

CHAPTER 13 CONTROL

The Kingdom

" It was a masterful plan. All it required was a large body of willing volunteers to carry it through, under the direction of a steering committee .... Many months hard toil lay ahead of them, with plenty of difficulties to overcome ...."   *The Six Trees*

This story is all about God's plan for establishing His Kingdom, His rule, and about our part in that plan, doing the work He has ordained for each one of us and for His church. As Peterson put it, God is in the driving seat, not us. He has the map of the route to the destination He has set for His world, His church and His children. We are contributing passengers, doing our bit to move the vehicle to its final destination. We navigate our way along the route, and the best way to do this, at all times, is under His direction. Even if our contribution is simply to sit and worship Him, it is enough. In fact, that is the best we can do. It is doing nothing that God will not indulge us in, because He knows how much we need the fulfillment of doing His will.

Returning to Matthew's gospel, 16:28 - 17:1. *"Some of you standing here are going to see .... the Son of Man in kingdom glory. Six days later, three of them saw that glory."* 'The Message'. It wasn't until I read Peterson's version that the juxtaposition of these two events dawned on me. I had always puzzled over the meaning of Jesus' remark to His disciples that some of them would not taste death until they saw the *"Son of man coming in his kingdom"*. He clearly did not mean that they would stay alive until the second coming, but I didn't link it with the transfiguration, because none of the texts I had read up to that time brought out that link so dramatically as Peterson does. As a result, something else also becomes clearer; the immediacy of the kingdom. It is for the present, not the far distant future. The second coming may be ages away, we don't know. Our full entry into heaven is at the end of our lives, for some of us that will be soon, for others, it will be many many years hence. The kingdom is for now, for this very minute and we can all grasp it, should all be within it.

We use this term very loosely though. What exactly is implied by the kingdom of God? Firstly, it is not, as English connotations of the word imply, simply the lands and country of a ruling monarch. The term has a broader application than that, encompassing rule, reign and authority, all words we routinely use in reference to God. The Jews of the Bible times recognized that God rules the universe and they regularly prayed for the day when He would reign in the world, unchallenged by idolatry and disobedience. They associated this with the coming of the Messiah. We Christians, of course, acknowledge Jesus to be that Messiah and because of His coming, we hold the belief that the kingdom has now been ushered in. But it goes further than that. God is not content just to have His kingdom introduced, and then leave it at that. The introduction precedes the consummation or completion of His master plan. We talk of God's plan of salvation, but the entry point for the rule of the kingdom in the heart, mind and life of each believer is only the first part of the master plan. The rest involves the outworking of God's law in our lives.

It is God's greatest desire that this should happen throughout His church, in order that His purposes for the church and the world may be entirely fulfilled. One word sums this up, - perfecting. This is God's work within us. Oswald Chambers sees it thus :- "A Christian worker has to learn how to be God's man or woman of great worth and excellence in the midst of a multitude of meager and worthless things. .... All of God's people are ordinary people who have been made extraordinary by the purpose He has given them. .... God is at work bending, breaking, molding, and doing exactly as He chooses. And why is He doing it? He is doing it for only one purpose - that He may be able to say, *"This is My man, and this is My woman."* .... Let Him have His way." Let God be in control of you, perfecting you and turning you more and more into the person He designed you to be.

Chapter 13 Control

The Law

"He's young, a bit shy socially, but get him onto Biblical subjects and he waxes lyrical and knowledgeable."   Two Churches

As He says in *Set Three* of the *'Words'* : *'My law is absolute. ..... Walk in it'*. The book of Psalms starts with this same idea *"Blessed is the man who does not walk in the counsel of the wicked or stand in the way of sinners or sit in the seat of mockers. But his delight is in the law of the Lord, and on his law he meditates day and night."* Psalm 1:1-2 Two things stand out here to me. One is to do with attitude and the other is all about behaviour. Blessed is the person who has his attitude correctly aligned, by taking delight in the law of the Lord. Blessed is the person who acts upon this attitude and meditates upon that law, day and night. They are both fairly demanding. The first because again, it runs counter to basic human nature. We tend to kick against rules. Our natural independence does not like being told what to do. Not only are we being told here that we must not be like that, but we are being shown that more than passive acceptance of it is required. We need to positively delight in the law! Some parts of it of course, we are only too willing to delight in, others we stick at. They face us with things about ourselves we would rather not face. With God's help though, even this can be overcome.

Meditation, we saw earlier, has many benefits. In our action packed lives we may be able to find a slot, perhaps once a week, or on an occasional retreat weekend for some deep, sustained meditation on a verse or two of Scripture. What is being proposed here is far more than that. It is a daily habit. This man makes the law the foundation of his thinking. It is in his mind all the time, whatever the circumstances he finds himself in. There is no simple one-for-all formula for doing this. Each person will find the method that suits them best. It takes determination, practice and discipline, but we are talking about walking by God's law, therefore we cannot avoid those three, none more than the last, discipline.

On the subject of discipline, a friend of mine was having some problems with her teenage children. She shared her difficulties with our fellowship group, saying that she really didn't feel she should bother God with her little worries. He had given her a perfectly good brain to sort out the problems and a strong enough personality to cope with the responsibilities of parenthood. That she wasn't coping was patently obvious to her and to the rest of us. The leader of the group gently took her to task. She should bring her problems to God, no matter how small. Not to do so is to exercise pride, but also, and he really stressed this, it is a matter of discipline. We have to school ourselves to open up to God minute by minute in all the vicissitudes of life, accepting His support and guidance thankfully.

He sets out His law in detail and clarity throughout the scriptures. Some parts are harder to understand than others I allow, and they are open to all sorts of interpretations, not all of which are helpful or correct. In this respect, I pray that I may not fall into error and ask your prayers for me and for all those whom God calls to be writers, or teachers and communicators of His word and will. We need those prayers, constantly, we are only fallible, weak human beings, not some kind of super race with all the answers.

As it has been said, walk in the known will of God and leave the unknown to Him. There's more than enough to get our heads round in what He has said, without fretting over things He has not explained or told us about. There is also sufficient in the scriptures to guide us in any and every circumstance, provided we are open to God's leading and prepared to accept His instructions, even when they seem unpalatable. Remember too, that this command is followed up with the promise that by walking in obedience to His law, *'you will prosper and know peace.'* What more could you ask, and what could be better? Let us dedicate ourselves to allowing the rule of God's kingdom to invade our entire beings and pervade the whole of our church life, in order that it can be ushered in more and more widely throughout all parts of the world.

CHAPTER 13 CONTROL

Surrender!

"Happy in his willing service to his Divine Master." 　　　　　　The Crusader

A lot has been said so far on the subject of surrender. It can never be enough. It is the answer to so many questions. How do we respond to God's call? By surrendering to Jesus. How do we walk in His law? By surrendering to it. How do we do God's work? In surrender to Him. How are we equipped for service for Him? Through surrender to His will and His enabling. There is a saying - 'God does not call the equipped, He equips those He calls!' This is absolutely true. You do not have to be fully trained and bristling with qualifications before God will use you. You only have to be surrendered. The training follows, in the school of life! As Oswald Chambers said, "Unless we have the right purpose intellectually in our minds and lovingly in our hearts, we will very quickly be diverted from being useful to God." I really appreciate the inclusiveness of that statement. There is a tendency in some Christian circles to over-elevate the heart at the expense of the intellect. Both are given to us by God, for His use. When I was first called to my career as a writer, I felt I had to be very careful not to be too intellectual. Then God whispered to me, 'don't be afraid of your intellect, surrender it, use it for Me. ' That was tremendously liberating. He made me the way I am, He intends me to work for Him, as I am, not in some other way that would be false for me! It is the same for you too. God will use you as you are, because He made you as He wanted you to be, and as you are you can carry out the tasks He has assigned to you. Chambers continues; "We are not workers for God by choice. .... We have to be in God's hand so that He can place others on the Rock, Jesus Christ, just as He has placed us." There in a nutshell is what it is all about.

Surrender is a vital piece of the Christian's kit. Why is so little preached on the subject I wonder? Admittedly, I'm not always the most attentive listener when the sermon is being preached, but I haven't heard much about this recently. I've heard loads of really encouraging stuff and some outstanding teaching on other issues, but only one memorable talk on surrender. It's not very popular or fashionable I guess. Thirty or so years ago, when I first became a Christian, you could hardly enter my church without falling over it, so to speak! We've grown up since then, I suppose and we no longer need such basic material. Nonsense. There is never a time in the Christian's life when they do not need to surrender to God and there has never been a time like the present for preaching and teaching on the subject, whenever that present is, 2003 or 2023.

To end this section, and the chapter, I'd like to take a little look at the *'Words'* in their entirety from the viewpoint of our need to surrender. *Set One* could be seen as 'pinning your colours to the mast', joining the Christian enterprise. The detail then has to be worked out, all your life, through the four other areas highlighted by each set of *'Words'*. *Set Two* asks for your response to the Lord's love. This is a surrender of your heart, your submission to His love for you. *Set Three* commands obedience to His law, starting the process of making your life pure, holy, righteous. This is the surrender of the will, perhaps the hardest of them all. *Set Four* calls for your dedication to the Lord's service, your surrender to the work He has lined up for you alone to do. This too requires submission of your will to His. Finally, *Set Five* deals with specific issues, and concerns your mindsets and lifestyle, all of which need to be brought firmly under His control, in order that your life and work may bring glory to Him.

CHAPTER 13 CONTROL

Broken Cisterns

"Sammarah had just bought a property that gave her control over the water supply to an entire valley. She diverted this source of power and sustenance into the grounds of her own estate, to create a 'paradise' garden for people to enjoy. People, that is, of her own choice" Sammarah's Garden

Jeremiah wrote of the situation in his time; *"Be appalled at this, O heavens, and shudder with great horror," declares the LORD. "My people have committed two sins: They have forsaken me, the spring of living water, and have dug their own cisterns, broken cisterns that cannot hold water." Jeremiah 2:12-13* This is exactly what we are doing when we adopt any other way than the Way of God, shown to us so clearly by our Lord Jesus Christ. Could it be that we are in danger of strangling the church by our own actions? Which would you rather be a part of? An institution destined for obscurity, or a powerhouse for God, a church that is alive and reverberating with God's praise and power? We might have to lose a bit of face and move out of our comfort-zones, in order to show the world that the church is not dead, but is alive just as it was in Acts and has a gloriously relevant message for the world.

We have seen God's intentions for His church in Acts, and in Jeremiah we see the sort of pursuits that please, or displease God. When we appropriate the church for ourselves, by seeing it as primarily there for the comfort and well-being of the members then we no longer allow the church to fulfil its God-given destiny and purpose. Once the church becomes ours rather than His, it loses its effectiveness and its power and becomes simply another human institution serving humanistic ends. I probably do not need to remind you that this book is entitled 'No Other God'. We cannot serve humanism. We can only serve God. It is time to openly acknowledge the full leadership of God over the church and His ownership of all that the church is and does. If this brings us into conflict with worldly leadership, then so be it. We are back at the debate in Chapter 9 about the work of the church, where we examined the question *'Why are you so preoccupied with the social when you should be focused on the spiritual?'* except that here we are discussing our aims rather than our focus. This is entirely right. Aims arise out of focus. Focus drives aims, not the other way round. If we have adjusted our focus precisely according to God's instructions, then our aims will fall into line properly. We are being recalled to this because it is so important, we cannot afford to overlook it.

In the story *'Sammarah's Garden'* we see the results of misappropriation of control. The consequences of Sammarah's actions are dire, not just for the other residents of the valley, or even specifically for the boy and his family, but also for Sammarah herself. Outwardly, in the boy's vicious attack threatening her very life, and inwardly through the diminishing effect on her personality of her behaviour. We see her becoming brittle, angry, dissatisfied, driven, and isolated even though she is surrounded by other people. Turn from her devastated position in the final scene of the story and focus on Idral, who 'alone had the power'. What a stunning image of God he presents. Fully in control. Why do we seek other sources of control, or try to usurp God's position of authority? Why is it so difficult to surrender, to lay down our control and submit to His? I don't have a complete answer to that, I just know it is so and that we must be constantly vigilant to correct the independent tendencies that lead us to want to take charge all the time; submission to God is the only way to have full spiritual health and eternal happiness.

Again, we are dealing with hard, challenging material, but we cannot duck these issues. To do so, we belittle ourselves. God made us and called us to more than an easy, comfortable life topped off by an eternity of bliss in heaven. Don't mistake me, I'm looking forward to my eternal bliss, and so should you. I cannot expect a soft ride in this life though, none of us can. That we will always have comfort and strength from our loving heavenly Father when the going gets tough is indisputable. That much is demanded of us is also indisputable, but, that He equips those who come to Him in surrender is equally indisputable.

CHAPTER 14

" RENEWAL "

Introduction

No other god offers new life.

".... this new school was going to be good."   2 K. B.

As we focus on renewal, of the individual believer and of the church I would like to return to a passage we considered earlier, in respect of worship and of compromise. Paul tells us to *".... be transformed by the renewing of your mind."* Romans 12:2. I would love to see such a transformation taking place throughout the church in my land, even worldwide. What a revival there would then be! What a powerhouse the church could become, impacting on troubled communities, on poverty, injustice, and the other ills of our modern day society. Instead of carefully attempting to offend no-one, through political correctness and compromise, which only offer ineffective solutions, the church could move into the gloriously triumphant, victorious leadership throughout the world that God so desires.

"I want My church to reverberate with My praise and My power so that the world sits up and takes notice."

"I want to pour out My Spirit on you so that you can be My messengers, stewards and ambassadors in the world."

"Where are the prophets, teachers, evangelists and missionaries for this age?"

"My church is The Church triumphant, victorious .... know that we can never, never be defeated."

The church, with notable exceptions, seems to be in a rut, using outdated methods to carry out its God-given task. In fact, I would say, in too many instances, the church has lost sight of that very task. I have to be careful what

I say here. Criticism is the easy tool of those with nothing better to offer. There is much going on within individual churches and in little pockets of renewal that is good, or even very good, but God wants the best. *I* do not offer a better way, **God** does.

I also do not mean to imply that all church tradition is wrong, or not appropriate any more. There are tried and tested ways of working that are still the most effective, human nature having changed little since the time of Adam and Eve. Nevertheless, there is ample room for change and improvement in all churches I believe. Any such alteration, however, must be at the instigation of God's Holy Spirit. It may concern practical things like the moving of pews, or which song books to use, but more importantly it will undoubtedly concern deep areas of doctrine and spirituality that need bringing back into line with scriptural principles. The only way individual churches, dioceses or denominations can renew themselves in preparation for revival and a revitalised life of service to God is through deep, repentant prayer and by allowing the Holy Spirit to take the lead in all and any reformation. Revival cannot be manufactured at the will of the church, nor will it come as the result of man-made schemes and initiatives. Only God can bring revival to His church, and then, only when He sees that we are open and ready for it.

CHAPTER 14 RENEWAL

Renovation

"With this last bit of the work accomplished, the jigsaw was complete and the park was ready for its grand opening day."   The Six Trees

The stories abound with scenes of renovation, that of the park being the most obvious. At a first glance there would seem never to have been a less promising collection of bits of ground. Smothered in weeds, alongside an industrial estate, unwanted and neglected, it was in a sorry state. No wonder the council weren't prepared to tackle it! Yet there was huge potential there, as the T. V. lady saw. It just took a lot of work to release that potential, which is what the story is meant to demonstrate. It's a parable for the church. Can you think of any institution that is made up of more varied bits and pieces than the church? Think of the Chinese house churches and the Vatican and then everything in between and you begin to see what a wonderful institution the church is with all its different parts.

A small detail springs to my mind at this point, to do with the approach of the T. V. lady to the problem. Having been sent for, she "turned up two weeks later, looked at the plots, considered the draft ideas .... went back and looked more closely at the plots then went away. After an interminably long fortnight, she came back to them with an innovative idea of her own ...." She did not come up with an instant answer to the problem. This is another parable within a parable. When we seek revival for the church, what should we do first? Pray. Then having prayed, we may have to be prepared to wait for God's response. This does not mean our prayers 'have not worked'. He alone knows the perfect answer and the perfect timing for that answer.

Notice too, the lady looked at the ideas of the people. We will all have our ideas about how the church should change. God does not cast those ideas aside dismissively. He listens and gives them His attention. How much do we listen and attend to Him?

The T. V. lady came up with a more innovative idea, imaginative and inclusive. I somehow think God has His better idea for the church. I read in a diocesan news sheet recently that this particular diocese is giving time and resources to considering the way it could re-shape itself. On the agenda for the discussions were four main topics; use of buildings, good old finance, deployment of clergy and outreach. Reading on it became obvious that outreach had a very low priority. All they are doing is shuffling the component parts of their 'park' around a bit. I know they will have said their prayers over this initiative. How much listening to and waiting on God have they allowed for afterwards? Have they let God come back to them with His perfect, masterful plan? I do not know, but I think not. If evangelism were central to their plans, then I think we would see a hugely different set of priorities and a diocese set on deep repentance, surrender and renewal, ready to move forward in the strength of God to take His word out in healing power to all parts of the communities it serves. Maybe I'm being uncharitable. Maybe this diocese is so minded and this is not evident from the news sheet.

Not that God won't bless them if it is not the case. That's the beauty of our God. He loves us so much, He desires to bless us at all times, however little we are doing for Him. We limit the flow of blessing by our reluctance or downright refusal to do things His way, and I'm no better than anyone else in this respect. So, we need renovation, not just re-shaping, a total overhaul, not just a bit of tinkering with the externals.

Individually and as a church, we need to allow God deep into our lives so that He can pour out His Holy Spirit upon us, as He longs to do, to burn out and soak away all that is not of Him, and fill the resulting vacant space with the works of the Spirit. That way we will truly reach out to our communities and become a force for good within them. As in the park, there is a lot of work to be done, but we need to make sure we are actually doing the right work.

CHAPTER 14 RENEWAL

Restoration

"Out of the ashes of worldliness and defeat arose the fire of effectiveness, spreading the wonder and power of the Lord to all it touched."

Two Churches

Renewal is a radical and comprehensive process. It is not like a television make-over programme, conducted at break neck speed over an impossibly short space of time, creating an instant impression and, sometimes literally, papering over the cracks. It is a loving, careful restoration that God longs to achieve in us. *"So here's what I want you to do, God helping you: Take your everyday, ordinary life - your sleeping, eating, going-to-work, and walking-around life - and place it before God as an offering. Embracing what God does for you is the best thing you can do for him. Don't become so well-adjusted to your culture that you fit into it without even thinking. Instead, fix your attention on God. You'll be changed from the inside out. Readily recognize what he wants from you, and quickly respond to it. Unlike the culture around you, always dragging you down to its level of immaturity, God brings the best out of you, develops well-formed maturity in you."* Romans 12:1-2 "The Message" Peterson really brings out the emphasis of this passage. It is so easy to fit in without even thinking about it. Our culture has an enormous influence upon us. Once we lived in what was known as Christendom, when our laws and society were founded entirely upon Christian principles. Now we live in a post-modern world, whatever that means, and our society is regulated in any way that seems best to those in authority, without obviously seeking any Divine guidance in the matter. This will not do for the Church though, as an institution representing God on earth. The Church, and each individual member, should be governed entirely, and visibly, by God's holy law.

As an encouragement, let us just take a peek at a church that did get its heart and mind right for God. I'm talking about the 1st Century church, as seen in Acts 2:42-47. A scan through the passage shows that they were devoted, filled with awe, united, generous, faithful, worshipful and thankful. Their activities included teaching, fellowship, breaking bread and prayer, they shared everything they possessed, went to the Temple daily and ate together in their homes. They met publicly, thereby giving a clear message to their society about who they were and what they believed. They taught the gospel fearlessly, without compromise. And the outcome of all this? They enjoyed the favour *'of **all** the people'* and *'the Lord added to their number daily those who were being saved.'* How much favour does the church find today with the people? Very little. Yet the church is desperately canvassing the favour of the people through its compromises with the world. Is there a connection, do you think, between this lack of favour and the fact that the church as a whole does not stand up for what it really believes in? People are very quick to spot inconsistencies. When the church behaves in ways that are contrary to what it teaches, given that its teaching is scriptural, those outside the church are understandably confused and critical. That is no reason to turn away from Biblical truth and conduct the affairs of the Church in accord with the ways of the current culture. The church must transform the age, not the other way round. We belong to the institution of which Jesus said *"the gates of Hades shall not prevail against it" Matthew 16:18* While this has in no sense ceased to be so, the line of defence has drawn out ever so thin in this generation. The church has survived so much opposition and persecution over the centuries, but is threatened by defeat from indifference and apathy within right now. God won't allow it to be totally overcome I am certain, but neither will He allow the current situation to continue.

CHAPTER 14 RENEWAL

Release from bondage

"Then he is filled with a great longing to find his mother's grave, ... He hurries to the churchyard, scouting round for the family graves. It is there. .... Bending to murmur his love and say sorry he knew what he'd do now with the rest of his life. He entered a Monastery, took his vows and in time became an Abbot. He gave many years loving and willing service to God and to the communities where his Monasteries stood, " The Crusader

Individuals are subject to many forms of bondage and it is an area that is amply covered in other literature and through the church's healing ministry. I am going to consider one specific bondage that I believe the church itself needs freeing from. This is denominationalism. It may seem strange to view this as a bondage but in some ways it is. It has been more usual to think of it as a sin, especially where it is manifested as fanaticism, where it is driven by pride or where it leads individual churches into antipathy. However, some churches are not free to follow Jesus and respond to the needs of this generation because their tradition has entrenched them into inflexible habits and procedures that they now exist to uphold. This is not a problem specific to certain denominations either. It can, and does occur right across the board in differing ways and to varying degrees. I do not feel it is my place to pinpoint any specific instances. If you are in such a church, you will more than likely be well aware of the situation. I can only encourage you to pray and trust that God will move your church on.

There is a danger that some of our schemes to remove denominational boundaries in order to work together more efficiently, are going to flounder on misplaced enthusiasm for the scheme itself rather than for the purpose for which it was conceived. The result being that we are sometimes wasting time and energy because we are tied into ensuring we are not being denominational. During the Second World War all sorts of unexpected alliances formed between neighbours because people forgot their differences in pulling together against the common enemy. When the church pulls together against its enemy, Satan, the differences cease to matter. They do not cease to exist, they are simply reduced to their correct perspective, serving to make the church a composite body, in which all people can find a niche, where they can be nurtured and grow in the Lord, according to their unique personality.

This business of denominations is a thorny one, beset with misunderstandings. One way of coming to terms with it is that, as with all of history, God has allowed the situation. He has not prevented them growing up within His church. Whether they were part of His original plan for the church I do not know, maybe they were. The reason I say that is based on Paul's words to the Corinthians, regarding the body :-

> *"Now the body is not made up of one part but of many. ..... God has arranged the parts in the body, every one of them, just as he wanted them to be. If they were all one part, where would the body be? As it is, there are many parts, but one body. .... God has combined the members of the body and has given greater honour to the parts that lacked it, so that there should be no division in the body, ... Now you are the body of Christ, and each one of you is a part of it." 1 Corinthians 12:12-27*

We are more accustomed, I suggest, to applying this to the situation within individual congregations. We are all different, each single one of us, we tell ourselves, we must praise the Lord for our differences and learn to get on together in this church. Because we are so familiar with this passage in that context, some of us have lost sight of its broader application to the entire church, with all its denominations. For eye, you could read, say, Roman Catholic. For hand, Baptist, for ear, Pentecostal, or whatever you like. Each branch has its identity, but that does not reduce its contribution to the church's great commission. Neither does it constitute a reason for separatism or for attempting to absorb all denominations into one amorphous blob, which would produce a characterless church that met no-one's needs. It may well be politically correct, but you know my opinion of political correctness by now, or you should! It's a case of all having the same aim, whilst maintaining our differing characteristics and dedicating those characteristics to the successful completion of the task.

Chapter 14 Renewal

New ways

"soon the question arises of which church, or churches, to encourage these new converts to join, so that they can be nurtured in their new found faith. .... For the bulk of the new Christians though, no church was found, readily available."
Two Churches

So far we have identified two key purposes for the church that need renewal, worship and evangelism. I would like to add a third here, that of discipling. Worship, as we have seen, is distinct from praise, and is the surrender of your entire life, physical, mental, emotional and spiritual, - *"a living sacrifice, holy, acceptable to God, which is your reasonable service."* Romans 12:1 NKJ. In the *'Words'*, Set Five E refers to worship and praise - *"I love to receive the praises of My children as they worship Me with hands and arms raised high,"* or even doing the conga, as happened at Spring Harvest one year!

Returning to another extract from the *'Words'*, the Lord asks *".... why are so few of you willing to seek My forgiveness on your knees, ...?"* Sinking to our knees in prayer or worship is easy, except for those with medical problems. The next bit is more challenging though - *"even flat on your faces"*. Two memories come to my mind here. One is of a teaching colleague of mine from many years ago. She was aware that I had recently had a conversion experience and that something extraordinary had happened to me.

"I hope you don't start going to extremes," she grumbled. It was a church school, so I suppose she was concerned for its reputation! "Not like the Curate at my church. The lady doing the flowers went in the other day and nearly fell over him, he was laid out flat on his face with his arms outstretched in the sanctuary. That's altogether going too far."

I have actually been flat on my face before the Lord, on one occasion, when taking part in a Christian dance week some years ago and this is the second memory. I don't really know how to describe the experience. Embarrassing at first, but with everyone else in the group also flat on their faces, that soon faded as we lost ourselves in worship. It was uplifting, even though I was physically down as far as I could go. The Lord wants this for us all, *"so that I might forgive and raise you up to walk even more upright lives ...."* Repentance is inseparably linked with worship. It is a key initiating element for renewal. If we wish to renew our worship, as I truly believe God longs for us to do, we cannot avoid repentance. Singing a few more songs in the minor key, or more reverently may lead us into true worship and repentance, but they do not constitute true worship and repentance.

I don't think I need say a lot here about evangelism. It is a dominant thread running throughout all that has already been said. There has been tremendous opening up and change in the area of worship, with things like the charismatic movement, the renewed acceptance of the need for 'baptism' in the Holy Spirit, which has swept through all branches of the church and the growth of powerful, Spirit-filled events like Spring Harvest, New Wine, Soul Survivor and so-on. Evangelism, for some churches, regardless of denomination, has become a top priority, but it is still an area desperately in need of regeneration, which we can seek wholeheartedly if we have a mind to and which God will restore in His time.

Thus we are left with the other key area of the church's business that I believe needs attention, that of discipling. This to me, is the one that has been most neglected in the last few decades. Refer back to the story *'Two Churches'* If tomorrow there was a huge evangelistic crusade throughout Britain, mightily blessed by God, with hundreds of thousands turning to Him and giving Him their lives, [I wish!] how would the established churches cope with the ensuing influx? They would be swamped. So what do we do? Pray that God will not send renewal, because we can't cope with it? I think not. I am certain God will raise up churches and people as the need arises. Those of us who are already Christians will need to be open-minded and welcome the new ways of 'doing church' that will inevitably be the outcome of this.

CHAPTER 14 RENEWAL

Transformations

"At the end of the day, everyone declared it a success and the town had a lovely park, presided over by the Horse Chestnut tree, to enjoy for years and years to come."
The Six Trees

Permit me to share something from the book *"The Heavenly Man"* by Chinese Pastor, Brother Yun. Yun has just been released from his second period of imprisonment. "The Lord told Deling [his wife] and me to leave everything, climb a mountain near our village, and seek God for his direction for our lives. My wife suggested that the training of young leaders was the most pressing need for the Chinese church. I agreed with her. But I knew there was so much work already waiting for me to join. Within days of my release one house church leader had already scheduled many meetings for me. Another brother invited me to travel with him to many different provinces, training and strengthening the churches. Yet another brother was starting a discipleship training school and he wanted me to come and help." Can you see the potential danger for burn-out here? All those pressing demands for the attention of the one brother, because there was no one else to do these tasks. The small band of leaders were stretched to breaking point coping with the constant influx of new converts, not least because they kept getting thrown into prison for their faith by the communist authorities. So how did they deal with the problem?

"After one week of fasting and prayer, I suddenly heard the Holy Spirit tell me these words, "Oil Station". When the Lord returns his followers must have oil burning in their lamps. He showed us that the oil of the Holy Spirit is the greatest need of this generation. We need to train workers who were able to carry the presence of the Lord with them wherever they went. The Lord Jesus made his will clear to us. There were many empty vessels in China," for China you could just as well read Britain , "but not enough carriers of God's oil to fill them up." There are thousands upon thousands of empty vessels in our land desperate for the filling of God's word and love. It is our task to pour out the oil God gives us into these empty vessels, in order that they may be nurtured and grow into fine, strong Christians, ready to spread the word even further. In Yun's words; "Without good training the light of God in our midst would gradually be extinguished." What a dreadful thought. It is reminiscent of God's words to the Ephesian church in Revelations; *"If you do not repent, I will come to you and remove your lampstand from its place."* Rev. 2:5 Tough talking, but these are tough times. We need to toughen up, get real with God and throw ourselves wholeheartedly into the task He has set before us, readying ourselves for a huge sea-change of revival that will sweep through our lands and bring thousands pouring in through the doors of our churches.

The church has to rise to the challenge of this situation, not through political correctness, or by fitting in to current climates of thinking. It is not the job of the church to affirm the state, or to trot along in the wake of the government, bemoaning the fact that religion is less and less significant in people's lives and church attendance is steadily falling. It is the church's ordained place and duty to take a stand at the forefront of the nation's life and give the lead in what to do on all issues, whether they appertain to social justice, to crime, to economics or anything else. On all these concerns, God has supplied answers through His word, the Bible. He has then raised up His church to provide teaching and nurturing so that people can find their way to Him, and then conduct their societies in such a way as to obey His sovereign law and bring glory to Him. When the church neglects this duty and dissipates its energies in other pursuits, then at the least its light becomes faint, but at the worst it goes out. I don't believe God will allow the latter to happen. He has set His church on earth to fulfil HIS purposes, not ours and He will do so.

I believe the Lord is giving us, in these *'Words'* a blueprint for our response to the challenge. I implore you not to dismiss it, or treat it lightly. We are immensely privileged that God should communicate with us in this way, setting out His intentions and wishes so clearly, in order that there should be no ambiguity or confusion. Let our response be only that which would please Him. The time is near, when the Lord will raise up His church in a mighty wave of renewal throughout this land. Are we readily available for it?

CHAPTER 15

"REBELLION"

Introduction

There is no other god.

"He is constantly in trouble. The authorities have run out of patience with him and deal with him harshly, when they can apprehend him, which only makes the situation worse and him angrier still."   Sammarah's Garden

We have said no other god can satisfy all our needs, no other god provides for us as our God does, no other god is in control and no other god offers new life. For this chapter, we will remember simply that there is no other god, all 'other gods' are in fact, false gods.

It may seem wrong to finish on such a negative theme as rebellion, but we all rebel. Nevertheless, as a close friend of ours said to comfort me when one of our children was being particularly rebellious, 'Never mind, Liz, God has been dealing with rebellious sons since time began!' Sheba son of Bicri, 2 Samuel 20, was a troublemaker fond of blowing his own trumpet, who rebelled against King David, the authority ordained by God. He lost his head as a result. Jeroboam goes down in the records, because he *"rebelled against his master"*, King Solomon, *2 Chron. 13*. God routed him, struck him down and he died. Samuel has this to say to Saul - *"For rebellion is like the sin of divination, and arrogance like the evil of idolatry. Because you have rejected the word of the Lord, he has rejected you as king." 1 Sam. 15:23* It wasn't just the ancient Israelites who were a 'stiff-necked' people either! Take a look at the Pharisees opposing Jesus. Rebellion is a serious matter with serious consequences. Moses' rebellion prevented him entering the promised land, although of course it did not preclude his entry into heaven, Matthew 17:3.
Every one of the stories has at least one rebel. Through detailed study of some of them, we shall see that rebellion is volitional, not instinctual, that it is not

age-related and that it is destructive. Dealing with it is a waste of resources that should be used to save the lost.

Yet there is a seductive attraction in rebellion. We enjoy the kudos of being a rebel, a daredevil. During childhood and the teenage years, rebellion is perhaps a little more understandable. After this it becomes regressive. In the *'Words'* it is referred to as our *'selfish, sinful ways'*. Our pursuit of *'other lovers'* is a form of rebellion. The fact that God has to say *"I expect you to obey ...."* implies that we prefer to rebel rather than obey. The lack of fulfillment of His creation is due in no small part to our rebelliousness. He roundly condemns the sin that has *"beset and spoiled too much of the work"* of the church, which often arises out of rebellion.

There may be all sorts of external pressures on us to rebel and no-one is exempt from such pressure but, hard though this is to accept, external circumstances do not govern our behaviour. We do. The only thing to blame for bad behaviour is the person behaving badly. We imagine that by altering the context, behaviour will change. It doesn't work because it is an ineffective strategy. It simply moves the problem into a different environment. Although this may sound merciless, I must say that I am a champion of tough love. It is not merciful, nor loving to condone rebellion or to imply that it is acceptable because of specific circumstances. God does not do this and neither should we, His children. When we choose to rebel, that choice is the only thing we do first. From then on, God steps in and everything else we do is in response to His intervention, either to dig ourselves deeper in or to remedy the situation. Our responses continue to be volitional. Not responding at all is a negative choice, by the way.

CHAPTER 15 REBELLION

Sam

"Sam's experiment was about to tell him what he wanted to know. What happens if....? Scowling deliberately, he snatched his exercise book up from the table, letting the broken pieces of the third pencil drop to the floor. He swaggered over to Mrs Brown and shoved the book onto the table in front of her, taking care to crease the pages." 2 K. B.

Let us take a step by step analysis of how Mrs Brown deals with Sam's rebellion. We may learn something to our benefit. Keep in mind the thought that she constantly enables Sam to comply before she instructs him, by setting up a context for obedience. All along it is his choice whether he complies or continues in rebellion. Bear in mind also that she has the interests of the rest of the class to consider, just as God has the whole church to consider, plus the rest of the world, as well as the needs of each of His children. Sam's behaviour has unsettled the other children, creating an atmosphere of tension and insecurity. She starts by calling him over to her, making the situation safe again by taking firm control. At the same time she instructs him to bring his work. There's no threat, it's a calm invitation. In a similar situation I would probably have bellowed something across the classroom a bit like this - "Come here, young man. I want a word with you!" which would have brought me straight into confrontation with Sam. Mrs Brown gets exactly what she wants though, and ignores the secondary behaviours, the swaggering, scowling etc. They are diversions. In the same way, God can penetrate whatever little distractions we throw up against His work in our lives, cutting right through to the heart of the matter.

When Sam arrives at her table and shoves his screwed up book under her nose, again, she does not reward the inappropriate behaviour with any but the most minimal attention. She smoothes the pages. Try smoothing a creased page with your hand. It flattens out, but the imprint of the creases remains. This is a powerful image for God's handiwork. Whatever bad things, including rebellion, litter our past, God can and will smooth away the effect. He does not annihilate or obliterate it entirely. The memory tends to remain, but without its sting. Rebellion is wrong, a sin. Recalling it, or facing up to it, will be uncomfortable. Confessing it and repenting of it brings God's smoothing hand to bear on it, rendering it powerless.

Although aggressive and resentful Sam was beginning to open up to Mrs Brown. He was more used to a chain reaction sequence in which he did something outrageous, got shouted at or worse, became surly and rude, leading to more stringent punishment, leaving him sulking and resentful, believing himself justified in his rebellious behaviour since 'this was how they treated him'. Mrs Brown breaks right through his pre-conceived notions, making it possible for him to start confronting himself and his own attitude rather than getting on the usual treadmill. Similarly, very often God intervenes with the unexpected to cause us to re-examine what we're doing, re-focus our attitude and re-adjust our behaviour.

The next strong image is that of the vacant chair. Take a moment to meditate on that. It was no coincidence that it was right beside Mrs Brown. Similarly God always has a place for us right by Him, giving us a sense of peace and well-being, even when, as in *Set Five D*, He moves us out of our comfort zones in order to achieve His purposes for us.

Finally, we have already discussed the control evidenced by Mrs Brown's hand resting on the back of the chair and Sam's consequent capitulation. She has still not told him off about the broken pencils, which, coupled with her unexpected approach has somewhat wrong-footed Sam. He had set up the situation, it's his behaviour that brings the sequence into play, but Mrs Brown is in charge and events are ordered by her, with Sam reacting rather than running the show. This is a new experience for him. We could sum up the sequence in the following way. We decide to act rebelliously. God calls us to come to Him. He smoothes the page, deals with the emotional or spiritual baggage we cart over to Him with our rebellion. He then offers us a place close beside Him. He reviews what we have done, praising the good, challenging us to move on, to do more for Him and providing the means to do it, including any necessary repentance, drawing us close to Him because that's where we can do our best and feel most secure.

Chapter 15 Rebellion

Jason

"The teenage son of one of those two middle-aged ladies, let's call him Jason, and his Mum, Sadie, is perennially in trouble, at school and with the police. At the very moment that Sadie is worrying her head over the fate of the far away Sierra Leoneans, Jason is being bundled into a Panda car having been apprehended with two friends, breaking and entering a local factory premises."

Two Churches

Rebellion is just selfishness Although the deepest desire of our hearts is to know God, we don't want to know His law. We are happy to know all the nice bits about God, His protection and blessings, but sometimes we don't want to follow His law, because it isn't always easy and we prefer the easy way. In this section we are going to look at some more strategies God uses in handling us in our rebellious moments. We need to turn to young Jason, and Chris the arresting officer. Here is a youngster for whom circumstances could well be cited as the reason for his rebellious behaviour. Firstly there's the environment, his immediate or close family is a fairly typical dysfunctional group, 'no visible Dad', a single Mum left to cope. Maybe she's in the throws of a mid-life crisis. Family all but gone, deserted by her husband, what is there left in life for her? All this could well be affecting Jason. Then there's the wider environment. The town, we know from the rest of the story, is lost, figuratively searching for spiritual meaning. The church is largely ineffective in reaching any other than its existing members, so no help from there for Jason, or even for his Mum.

Secondly, there's the peer group. We are very fond these days of laying all the blame for the misdemeanours of our youngsters at the door of 'the peer group'. But that group consists of others the same age who all have parents doing the same thing. In truth, which ones are the bad influence and which are the ones being led astray? Every member of that group has exactly the same amount of free will as all the others. None of them have to behave badly, run riot or whatever else they're doing to provoke a chorus of tutting from the elders of the community. I am not playing down the strength of these influences. It is hard for anyone, teenage or not, to stand against the mighty urge of those words, 'oh come on, every one's doing it', whatever 'it' is. I'm addressing those who belong to the kingdom of God here though. We know, absolutely, that we have a faithful God, who comes to our aid whenever we cry out to Him. In situations where influences are enticing us to rebel, or embark on patterns of behaviour that we know are wrong, our decision to refuse to follow the crowd or take a wrong step is strengthened instantly by the work of the Holy Spirit within us.

CHAPTER 15 REBELLION

Chris

"The older of the two arresting officers actually feels quite concerned over these youngsters, particularly Jason, ... It isn't the first time he's pulled Jason in and, although outwardly stern, he's inwardly exasperated that there's so little he seems able to do to steer the youngster onto better paths."

Two Churches

Chris gives us an insight into some of the ways in which God can and does intervene when His children rebel. As you can see, the sequence starts by establishing status. Chris as the senior, arresting officer, is in authority. So is God, let's be in no doubt about that. Secondly, it establishes attitude. Chris may be outwardly stern, but inwardly he cares enough to feel exasperated at how little he can do for Jason. God's attitude is one of care. Look at *Set One* of the *'Words'*. *"I want all men to know My love, **My care**, My salvation."* Although He condemns sin and rebellion God still cares about every one of us. Thirdly, it shows that there is a lot God can do without our full co-operation. Chris arrests Jason, which brings him under control and prevents him offending any further. God can do exactly that in any situation, to limit the damage. Never underestimate the capability of our God to work within seemingly hopeless situations. I am not arguing theoretically here by the way. Looking back over my life before I became a Christian, I can clearly trace the hand of God steering me, via situations, events and people, although I was largely unaware of it at the time. Neither is this something only for a lucky chosen few. We need to grasp hold of the fact that despite all appearances to the contrary, God has His purposes for absolutely every human being ever born. He will do all that He possibly can, and this is rather a lot more than we realise, to bring those purposes to fulfillment.

Next we see Chris escorting Jason home and explaining what's occurred to Sadie. God always escorts us, even if all He can do is be a shadowy figure on the periphery of our lives. Chris enlists help from Sadie as well as informing her. God has His agents, the Christian fellowship, whom He prompts to move alongside troubled and searching souls. How many times have you been grateful for the ministry of God delivered through a Christian friend? How many times has God moved you to be such a comforter? This is how the Christian family works, at its best, for itself and for the world.

Chris demonstrates something else about God in circumstances such as this. He shows us how frustrated God feels at being excluded from our lives when we rebel and will not co-operate. In my teaching career I've encountered children who seem aloof from all efforts to impact on their attitudes or behaviour for the better. In that human situation, I have had to concede defeat in one or two cases, because the child needed more specialised help than I could provide as a generalist classroom teacher. Thankfully God is never in that position! He is the specialist. We can always turn to Him when our meagre resources run out, and He will have more resources available than you or I could ever dream of.

Also, because Jason is excluding him from his life, Chris is prevented from appearing as anything other than stern. It may be that you know someone who can only see God as stern and forbidding. It may be that, even though you are a faithful church goer, this is how you view God. The reasons for this may be deep seated, perhaps a result of the parenting you received as a child. It need not be like that though. God is only stern with the sin, not with the sinner. He loves the sinner, but you cannot receive that love fully unless you open up to it, therefore you are seeing more of the sternness against your sin than of God's love for you. Remember, sin confessed and repented of is taken away by God, opening the way for His love to pour in. I urge you, if this describes your position or feelings, don't continue any longer in this sadness. Let God in. He will be gentle, although He will deal with whatever needs sorting in your life. It will be worth it though, I assure you.

Finally, we see Chris, very humanly, resorting to the comforts of a choc bar. I have to confess, that is one of my favourite bolt-holes in times of stress, hence my problems with my ever-expanding waistline! I can sympathise with him. All is not lost though. Corny though the next bit is - he and Rashid 'put the world to rights' - in fact, this is exactly what God does do, isn't it? He puts the world to rights, His way, if we let Him.

CHAPTER 15 REBELLION

The Trees

"The Oak tree took pride of place in the children's adventure playground, ... The Pine tree was pressed into service as one support for the climbing frame. The Silver Birch naturally took its place within the multi-sensory nature of the park, ... The magnificent Beech stood at the new entrance to the park, ... The Poplar was a bit of a problem, ... The direction of the path leading to the Poplar was altered to go past it and on towards the main player in the drama, the Horse Chestnut."   The Six Trees

In this final section I am going to examine the images presented by the trees and relate them to our consideration of rebellion. You could say that they provide manifestations of five aspects of rebellion; arrogance, disobedience, selfishness, defiance and resentment. The Beech gives us a picture of arrogance; the Silver Birch, as an interloper, represents disobedience, being where it shouldn't be; around the Horse Chestnut are all the choking weeds of selfishness; defiance is clearly evidenced in the whipping and lashing of the Poplar and what could appear more resentful than the lofty Pine. This leaves the Oak, which in contrast, portrays compliance and all things good. We see those same characteristics in certain people within the stories; arrogance in Sam, disobedience in Peter as a child, selfishness throughout Sammarah's life, resentment in the boy and defiance in Jason prior to his conversion. They are ugly images, but sadly, the human race is all too prone to them, nor are Christians exempt from them.

Figuratively we can see the effect of rebellion and its associated behaviours in the story *"The Six Trees"*. They create a wasteland. Dwell for a moment on the plot containing the Silver Birch. "A bit of scrubland .... left spare", neither productive nor attractive, giving house room only to "self-setters" that "had taken root there". Not the legitimate occupants of the plot. Just as rebellion is not a legitimate occupant of our time and energies, but is an interloper that we accommodate to our cost. The picture continues in similar vein, "some were vandalised, others did not prosper and this one was .... spindly and weak looking". A stark picture of how we are when we let sin and rebellion rule our lives.

The Poplar is a salutary example. It has its top chopped off! Similar to the Silver Birch, initially it is in the wrong place. A tree of the size it will attain on maturity is inappropriate for a small town garden. Ignorance caused the young couple to choose such a tree. They simply popped into their local garden centre, saw something that they liked the look of and impulsively bought it. They clearly did not do their homework to find out how big it would grow. It very quickly posed a threat, terrifying the young mother and forcing the couple to deal with it through drastic measures. There is an unconsidered impulsiveness about rebellion. It looks attractive, so with no more thought for the consequences, the rebel launches into it. Look at the Poplar in the gale though. It is whipping and lashing alarmingly. What a picture of the rebel caught up in the effect of their rebellion. Tossed this way and that restlessly, until someone or something terminates the action, painfully. It was some time before the truncated Poplar at last found its true place and knew peace. Only then could it grow and prosper. A few moments spent considering the outcome of deciding to buy that particular tree could have prevented a lot of trouble. A few seconds, a pause as long as a breath, may be all it takes to think 'no, I won't rebel, tempting though it is, I'll do God's will, like it or not and I know He will help me'. What a lot of heartache and pain could be avoided if we all adopted that strategy.

CHAPTER 15 REBELLION

The Horse Chestnut

"This tree completely eclipsed the fountains that had been intended as the central feature of the park"   The Six Trees

Imagine the devastation surrounding the beautiful Horse Chestnut tree, "the last bit of the park to be dealt with .... a large circular patch in the middle of the old 'horses' field, banked up to house height and covered with a further twenty or thirty foot growth". What a picture of entrenched stubbornness and again, look at the effect of it - "the mess that had reigned so long at its roots and that had threatened to defeat the volunteers ". They were in a real battle, just as we are in a battle, as God's army, fighting with Him to win the world for Him. Notice how weary and close to defeat they were. Notice how the "fair weather friends" have all fallen away, as they do. But this last little remnant of the volunteers refused to be overcome. In spite of their depression and depletion, they stuck at it and won the victory in the end.

Let us have a look at what was required of them for this to be achieved. The key is in the word 'attack' and in the grammar. As I pondered on this story, I turned to my 'Oxford Practical English Usage', which is always to hand whenever I am writing. We first meet the key word at the start of the clearing process - "***They attacked*** it on all fronts, fast and furiously ". According to my book, the words in bold are in the simple past tense. "They attacked", pure and simple, no hesitating, no messing about. This tense is "often used with reference to finished periods and moments of time." They attacked - it is finished. Let's have an end to it, no more rebellion. Furthermore, this tense " is the 'normal' one for talking about the past". Let's make it our norm, to attack and rid ourselves always and promptly of sin and rebellion.

The second occasion we meet this key word is a bit later on, talking about the Horse Chestnut rising triumphant over the mess that had threatened the volunteers, "when **they came to attack** this last bit of desolation". Here we have the simple past, "they came" coupled with the infinitive, "to attack". There is a resolute purposefulness about their action. Infinitives, by definition, do not usually show actual times, referring to events in a more general way. The use of an infinitive here generalises the action against rebellion to all occurrences of it. There is no ambiguity here. The volunteers came for the specific purpose of attacking and clearing the mess. Rebellion is sinful and we should take swift, purposeful action, in God's power, whenever we encounter it.

They "set to once again" immediately after the discovery of the Horse Chestnut. Note the revitalised determination there. What had given their flagging spirits the boost they needed? It was the glimpse of that majestic tree. When we fix our inner, spiritual gaze on Jesus, the author and perfecter of our faith we are uplifted and renewed. Part of their battle was won at that moment and they received encouragement and strength for the last heroic struggle. Eventually, the Horse Chestnut rose "victorious and triumphant over the mess", just as God reigns over all.

Finally, look at the weapons they used in their fight. As well as hand tools, they brought in the heavy artillery. But note, it is only "*a* JCB" and "*a* dumper truck". One of each of those was sufficient. They didn't waste resources having six or a dozen of them. God provides exactly sufficient for the moment. They had lots of smaller tools, belonging to individuals. Each gave out of their plenty for the good of all. This is a good illustration of the twofold nature of the enterprise God is calling us to engage in. On the one hand there is His provisioning, on the other is our willingness. Put the two together and we, as the church are an invincible force within the world.

Epilogue

To sum up, I see the key premise of this book falling into five main points :-

1) That God loves everyone, whoever they are and that He wants everyone to be saved from the consequence of their sins, whoever they are. That He longs for everyone, whoever they are, to live eternally in an intimate, passionate relationship with Him.

2) That God has ordained His church here on earth to spread this Gospel message to all people everywhere.

3) That the church, in the main, has failed to do this as effectively or as well as it could. Consequently many hundreds of thousands of people are lost.

4) That God commands His church to repent of this failure and turn to Him in renewed determination to fulfil its true purpose on earth.

5) That He is giving us a blueprint here in these *'Words'* for recovery and action, which we ignore to our own detriment and to the detriment of the world.

It is not my intention, as I have already said, to attack the church. I am working as a channel for the Lord, to bring to the attention of as many people as possible within the church hierarchy, both high and low, ordained and lay, what God is telling us in these *'Words'* and what He requires of us in terms of response and action, right now at the start of the 21st century.

If we were to take a peep into the future for the two children in the story *"2 K. B."* it would be logical to say that Netta is going to engage with the chances she is being offered and become fully involved. She looks set to be a model pupil; in salvation terms, a model convert. Whereas Sam, we can see, is fighting a rearguard action, kicking against the system, determined not to cooperate, not to give up his independence and conform. In salvation terms, he is the worst model convert. In fact, he's not a convert at all, and we cannot really imagine he ever will be.

We are reckoning without two things though. One is, of course, the indomitable Mrs Brown. Remember her hand across the back of his chair? This teacher is one to be reckoned with. She has power because she has authority, and both are used to ensure the highest good of all her pupils. As I have pointed out, she is not God, but she does represent aspects of His character, none more than His power, authority and concern for our good.

So what is the second thing? Remember this observation of Sam's? "The children at his old school never lined up in this docile way ...." The second influential factor in the situation is the rest of the class, the other children. In their keen willingness to learn and to conform, Mrs Brown has a powerful ally. Taking the spiritual lesson from this, we can see that they represent the fellowship of believers. As with that fellowship, they are a mixed bunch, all with their individual needs, strengths and weaknesses. Together, though and all focused on the same goal, they constitute a strong force in the situation. Together with God, the church fellowship can be a tough partner in the work of salvation in the world. That is what God is telling us in these *'Words'*. Together with each other and together with Him, we can influence the world for the better.

The message of salvation through the death of Jesus on the cross is the same message for all mankind. Jesus' statement that no-one comes to the Father except through Him is for everyone. Jesus is the way God has ordained for people to be rescued from their sin and enter eternal life. God has not set up any alternatives, nor does He relax that ruling. This is how it is. Our differences colour how we receive the good news of salvation, but they do not alter the facts of salvation in any way whatsoever.

For our two children, if we indulge ourselves in a second peek into their future, the outcome could well be very different to that envisaged earlier. Netta, quiet, well-behaved, good and passive, may just be drifting along, doing as she's told, not causing any trouble, but in fact, not actively participating at all. Simply there for the ride, for what she can get.

Sam, on the other hand, who we have clearly seen to be bright and quick thinking, may well finish up the more involved of the two, more committed to the situation, to doing well for Mrs Brown, and for himself.

Either way, each of them has to make a decision about how to respond. It is the same in the Christian life. We are all given the same opportunity, but how we respond to it is a matter of personal decision. These *'Words'* are, above all else, a plea from God to all of us within the church to make a decision for Him and for the furtherance of His kingdom. The first priority of the church should be the overt spreading of the Gospel to every part of the world, in every possible manner and by all possible ways and means. Social work, aid and charitable work then assume their rightful place in the order of priority for the church, secondary to this first task, but in support of it.

At present there are little pockets of such activity, in all kinds of churches, regardless of denomination. God, I believe, wants all churches, regardless of their denomination, to make His work of evangelism their top priority and what is more, I believe He wants it now. There isn't time to say 'let's think about this, let's have a committee to consider all the angles'. While we hesitate and drag our feet, thousands of souls are lost and thousands live drab, meaningless lives without knowing God, without knowing the wonder and excitement of His fulfillment and His love. The situation is urgent. Forget all the urgencies of the world. This one is of eternity and it matters more than anything else ever can.

Do we care about that? Maybe we do, but maybe not enough. Maybe some don't see that they need to care. But God does, and He only has us, by His own choice, to tell people about Him and about the glorious salvation that is theirs in Jesus. The actual salvation of course, is His work. We only have to communicate it's availability. In fact, our task is relatively easy. Not so easy in areas where you are persecuted and tortured for doing it, but here, in the West, easy. So easy, we don't seem to bother doing it very much.

Now, may I leave you with some longer *'Words'* from our Lord God, given to me during the process of writing this book.

> *"My words carry My authority, the weight of Who I Am. They cannot be gainsaid. Because I have said it - so it will be, do not doubt this. I*

will tolerate no trivialization of or opposition to My word, there are consequences if you do not obey or if you refuse to accept, or treat My words lightly."

"When will you put the spiritual needs of the starving before their social needs? Don't you realise people are starving in spirit as well as in body? The world has enough politicians and aid agencies to see to its physical needs but it only has you to see to its spiritual needs. You must bring word of My salvation to the world. They cry out for nourishment for their souls and all you feed are their bodies. Feed their souls first and help feed their bodies afterwards.

Do not ask why dreadful things happen in the world - starvation, disease, oppression, cruelty. I stay My hand that more may come to know Me before I judge the world and condemn the evildoers and the evil one. I stay My hand, so that as many as possible may come to enjoy the assurance of My salvation. They are slow to come. They are so slow because you are slow to bring them My word, because they are not hearing about Jesus, My precious, beloved Son, who I gave for them.

They are not hearing because not enough of you are telling them about Him. Yet nothing else, nothing else in all the world, in all My creation, is as important.

You talk about worldly things as important, vital, essential, as though without them you would perish. What you do not realise, will not see, is that you are perishing, despite having the world.

Only one thing matters - that you should be saved; that all men may come to know My love and be saved, to have eternal life with Me in heaven.

This is what I ordain. This is My desire, what I want and what I command. This is My will. Walk in it and have no other god but Me."

REFERENCES

The author and publisher gratefully acknowledge permission to reproduce copyright material. Every effort has been made to trace and acknowledge copyright holders.

Brother Yun with Paul Hattaway   *"The Heavenly Man"* 2002 Pub. Monarch Books

Buchanan, A. *"God has feelings too"* 1986 Kingsway Publications Ltd.

Buchanan, A. *"Bible Meditation"* 1987 Kingsway Publications Ltd

Chambers, O *"My utmost for His highest"* © 1935 by Dodd Mead & Co., © 1963 by the Oswald Chambers Publications Assn., Ltd. Used by permission of Discovery Publishers, Box 3566, Grand rapids MI 49501. All rights reserved.

Cunningham, D. & Hamilton, L. Adapted from *"Why not Women?"* by Loren Cunningham & David J. Hamilton, published by YWAM Publishing, P. O. Box 55787, Seattle, WA 98155, and used with permission.

Eliot, T. S. Collected Poems 1909 - 1962 © 1936, by Harvourt Brace Jovanovich, Inc.; © 1943, 1963, 1964 by T. S. Eliot. Reprinted by permission of Faber & Faber Ltd.

Gass, B. & Gass, D. *"Teach your children"* in *"the Word for Today"* Wednesday March 5th 2003, UCB

Hughes, S & Greenslade, P. *"Every Day with Jesus : The Great Escape"* CWR, for Monday August 6th 200, used by permission of CWR

Hughes, S. *"Every Day with Jesus : The Names of God"* CWR, for Friday December 8th 2000, used by permission of CWR

Hughes, S. *"Getting the best out of the Bible ; A new look at Biblical meditation."* CWR 1989 used with the permission of CWR

Hughes, S., *"Christ Empowered Living"* CWR, 2003, Pages 187-188, used with permission of CWR

Hughes, S. *"Everyday with Jesus : The Names of God"* CWR Saturday 11th November; Tuesday 14th November 2000, used with permission of CWR

Hughes, S. *"Everyday with Jesus : Your Father and my Father"* CWR Tuesday 4th November 1997 used with permission of CWR

Kornitzer , M. *"Adoption"* 4th Edition 1973 Putnam & Company Ltd, London

Read, P. P. *"The Templars "* 1999 Weidenfield & Nicolson

Saint Augustine   *"Confessions"*   in Water, M. comp. "The New Encyclopedia of Christian Quotations"   © 2000 by John Hunt Publishing Ltd

Spearing, E. (trans.) *"Julian of Norwich : Revelations of Divine Love"* 1998 Penguin Books

Swan, M., Reproduced by permission of Oxford University Press from *"Practical English Usage"* © Michael Swan, 1980, 1995

The Archbishop's Council, *"The Order for the Celebration of Holy Communion"* Order One, 2000, Church House Publishing, London.

Yohannan, K. P. (Ed.) *"Send!"* Gospel for Asia News magazine, Vol 22 No 1 Jan / Feb 2002, Pp 5 - 9 & P 14; Vol 21 No 3 P 12; Vol 23 No 1 P 18.

Yohannan, K. P. *"Revolution in World Missions"* 2000 gfa books